T0171058

Create Space with Your Higher Self

Angelic Feng Shui

SERAFINA KRUPP

BALBOA
PRESS
A DIVISION OF HAY HOUSE

Copyright © 2013 Serafina Krupp.

All rights reserved. No part of this book may be used or reproduced by any means, graphic, electronic, or mechanical, including photocopying, recording, taping or by any information storage retrieval system without the written permission of the publisher except in the case of brief quotations embodied in critical articles and reviews.

Balboa Press books may be ordered through booksellers or by contacting:

Balboa Press
A Division of Hay House
1663 Liberty Drive
Bloomington, IN 47403
www.balboapress.com
1-(877) 407-4847

Because of the dynamic nature of the Internet, any web addresses or links contained in this book may have changed since publication and may no longer be valid. The views expressed in this work are solely those of the author and do not necessarily reflect the views of the publisher, and the publisher hereby disclaims any responsibility for them.

The author of this book does not dispense medical advice or prescribe the use of any technique as a form of treatment for physical, emotional, or medical problems without the advice of a physician, either directly or indirectly. The intent of the author is only to offer information of a general nature to help you in your quest for emotional and spiritual well-being. In the event you use any of the information in this book for yourself, which is your constitutional right, the author and the publisher assume no responsibility for your actions.

Any people depicted in stock imagery provided by Thinkstock are models, and such images are being used for illustrative purposes only.
Certain stock imagery © Thinkstock.
Angel painting by Serafina Krupp

Author Photo by Tom Sullivan, Newport Beach

Printed in the United States of America.

ISBN: 978-1-4525-7815-6 (sc)
ISBN: 978-1-4525-7817-0 (hc)
ISBN: 978-1-4525-7816-3 (e)

Library of Congress Control Number: 2013913030

Balboa Press rev. date: 8/7/2013

This book is dedicated to my loving dad and mom,
Carl Phillip and Marguerite Louise Purpero

Contents

Preface

The inspiration to write this book "Create Spaces with your Higher Self " came from all of my many experiences working with clients, friends, family, students, angels, and the saints. I have been doing interior design and practicing The Western thought of Feng Shui since 1985. Through my childhood and adult life I have been working with the angels. It made sense for me to combine working with the angels and Feng Shui. The formation of Angelic Feng Shui was the authentic way for me.

In my life I have always tried to become more aware or another way of saying this more conscious. Any insights on how to go about this I would embellish into my classes or workshops.

I discovered that when I felt self-conscious or would self- sabotage myself it was the covert critical inner child that was observing me.

To change this behavior I discovered that it was as simple as just internally saying to myself or saying out loud to myself I choose to observe myself right now from my higher self.

I found that the more I called on my higher self to be the observer the healthier my critical inner child became. Because of this practice it has become second nature to observe from my higher self. As a result of observing from my higher self this book is finally getting published.

I also changed the title of this book so everyone who reads this can choose to read this with their higher self and follow their bliss.

Through-out the book we will habitually call in the higher self. My desire is for you the reader to use this information and feel more joy, love, and light. It is my desire to share with you the reader my personal experiences, my knowledge of Feng Shui, and how to work with angels.

Angelic Feng Shui brings Feng Shui to another dimension. A dimension I have used my whole life, our connection with the spirit. When you add this dimension to your life you add the love and guidance of the Divine. The changes in your life are significant.

Through the practice of Angelic Feng Shui I have witnessed the transformation of people's lives. My clients have experienced healings, financial improvement, new found love, healed relationships, and blossoming careers. My students and clients start living their dreams. Their lives become filled with more joy! They find inner peace. They have the tools to re-script their lives and they make life changing choices. This results in Hugh transformations in their lives in a very short period of time.

This transformation creates a happier, more loving, fulfilled, human being. To aid in this transformation in the chapters of this book you will discover angels to call upon for all areas in your life. You will discover that there is angelic support and help for everything. I believe everyone has a direct line to heaven. Angels respond when you call them. They are a blessing. I feel everyone can do it. It just takes practice. Practice, Practice, practice and it will become natural for you to connect with the angels. We are in truth spiritual beings in a human body form. We don't need to learn how to become spiritual we already are spiritual. We need to learn how to become good human beings.........and the angels are there to help.

Angelic Feng Shui when properly practiced and given a chance creates balance and harmony in all areas of one's life. It brings balance and harmony to our mind, body, and spirit. It gives the inner peace that we need in this ever changing world.

To achieve this connection with spirit it takes an open heart, an open mind, and a willingness to truly want to connect. You need to want and feel it with your whole being. You will have an opportunity in each chapter of this book to do this. This book covers the spiritual areas of your life as well as the physical areas of your home/work environment. I will give you the correlating angels that relate to and help with the different areas. The angels we will be working with are guardian angels, archangels, cherubim, seraphim, and powers.

At the end of each chapter there is a meditation to assist you on your journey. Read and record the meditations with your own voice. Then close your eyes and listen to the recording. When you listen and the meditation is too fast go back and record again to adjust it to the right pace for you. You want to be able to be completely relaxed and enjoy.

Before writing this book I wondered what angels to include. I always ask the angels for a sign and as I arrived home from my walk one day there was a sloe of feathers on my front lawn. It was a clear sign to me that there would be many that would be included. I thank them all for all their help and support in writing this book.

My mother recently passed and gray feathers keep showing up. I know she is around and influencing me to put as much love and humor in this book as possible. Thanks mom.

Acknowledgments

I would like to thank my loving husband Marshall for always being there and giving me support. I would like to thank my sister-in-law Ruth for doing an incredible job of editing. I would like to thank my friend Candyce for reading it and for giving me the feedback on what she didn't understand so I could make it clear for the reader. Thank you to my friend Holly for helping me with formatting the book. I am in deep gratitude to the Angelic realm for their support, love, light, and inspiration.

Angelic Feng Shui

This book is about creating spaces with your higher self through "Angelic Feng Shui". It is about the teachings and practice of Feng Shui with Angelic help. The will book explain the nine different areas of your life that can be enhanced and re-scripted. It introduces the world of the Angelic realm that one can call upon to enhance the nine different areas in your life. It explains the Bagua Map, the Roadmap that is the map to your treasures in life.

The book also explains how important it is to choose what you truly desire and how powerful it is to choose the environment you want to live in. Because, what you choose to surround yourself with determines how you live your life and determines what you become. Your environment is an expression of who you are. Practicing Angelic Feng Shui you will become aware of the areas and treatments that will change your Health, Career, Fame, Wealth, and Relationships.

This book will introduce you to some of the Archangels, Angels, and the different groups of angels. I will share with you the endless possibilities that lie in store for you with these heavenly connections and help. They are messengers from heaven. They give us Truth, Wisdom, Love, Knowledge, Grace, Protection, harmony, healing, and Guidance. They guide us to the heavenly kingdom within each one of us. Everything you need to know, all the tools you need for changes are inside of you. This heavenly connection will unlock and open the doors of knowingness. For non-believers I challenge you to check it out and to surrender to the resistance and reservations.

With practice you can become sensitive enough to see, feel, or hear them. You will be able to imagine them, picture them and sense them as the Light beings they really are and who are just here to help you on your journey. There is a thin line between heaven and Earth. It is a matter of vibration. Right now with all the changes going on in the world there is so much help from the other side. The vibration of the whole planet is lifting, let's lift with it.

The message thread of this book is to empower you and give you the tools to create the spaces inside of you and to create the spaces around you that you want to live and work in. The deeper message of the book is to let you, the reader know that you are the main character in your life and that your world revolves around you. If you don't like the way things are you have the choice to change it.

Call upon the Angelic realm for help and they will guide you on how to start making choices that bring you joy! If you resist and are unable to surrender to the ability to manifest what you want, this book will guide you on how to re-script your life in your inner world and outer world. It will show and explain to you how we can create Heaven on Earth.

Using the principles of Feng Shui and the Angelic realm you will be able to create enlightened, positive, changes in your surroundings and your lives. Through the practice of Feng Shui you can achieve balance to the mind, body and spirit within the interior and exterior spaces of the world you create and live in. Feng Shui is about bringing in balance, the yin and the yang. Feng Shui is about bringing you to that place of inner peace.

I have written this Book to bring forth the practice of Feng Shui at an understandable and user-friendly level with the teachings, passion and sacredness of the cultures of the past and the sophistication, maturity, and needs of people in today's modern world.

My passion is to affect people's lives in a way so they can observe themselves from their higher self and experience their bliss. To give them tools to create beauty in the world they live in. To bring more love in their relationships. To create financial returns and abundance for all. My passion is to give you the tools to call in all your blessings!

Everyone has a choice of five paths on this earth journey that we are on. There are two lower paths, one middle path and two higher paths. With Angelic Feng Shui you will have the tools to choose your highest path. Let Angelic Feng Shui be the key for you to open your Golden door.

My wish is for you to open your heart and be ready to bring in more love, light, joy, and abundance into your life. I wish for you to experience your transformation easily, effortlessly, and joyfully. To begin your journeys just turn the page…….

From my Heart to your Heart……..………Serafina

Feng Shui and the Bagua Map

Feng Shui is all about energy and has been practiced for over 3,000 years. It is a Chinese term meaning "wind and water". The moving of air and the moving of water activates and invigorates energy. In Feng Shui we use the word Chi as the name for the energy around us. There are three principles of Feng Shui and these principles are: everything is alive, everything is changing and everything is connected. Feng Shui is also about balancing the dark and the light, the feminine and the masculine, and Yin and the Yang. It is about bringing harmony and balance to one's life.

In Feng Shui it is very important to combine together in our surroundings the right mixture of the elements; water, wood, fire, metal, and earth. We combine this perfect blend of elements into our environments by using nature as an example. It is important to bring this balance and beauty of nature into our lives. Feng Shui is about healing people and making them feel whole and healthy. Feng Shui is about healing people with themselves and with others.

To give you a clear understanding and a structure to formulate this thought we start with the Bagua map. The Bagua map is the foundation of Feng Shui. It is the most result-producing tool in Feng Shui. The Bagua map correlates with the design and structure of your home as well as it correlates with each individual rooms of your home. You can also use the Bagua map to correlate with the structure of your place of business, your desk, and your car.

Feng Shui is the Chinese art of placement. There is order in the universe and the Bagua map shows you the placement. It is the roadmap for the manifestation of change in one's life and environment. This tool aids in bringing the blessings of health, joy, and abundance into your life. When you follow the Bagua map guide obstacles fall away and powerful changes will occur in your life. You will be manifesting blessings in your life. The Bagua map is the major tool to re-script your life. It is the roadmap to your treasures in life.

To get started draw a floor plan of your home on an 8 1/2" x 11" piece of paper. Once you have drawn the floor plan of your living space, place a sheet of vellum paper over the floor plan and draw the Bagua map. Whatever the shape of your home is fit it completely inside the Bagua Map. The entire structure should be within nine sections. The Bagua is stretched to accommodate the shape of your home. Draw out the nine spaces and label the spaces as shown on the example of the students floor plan on the next page.

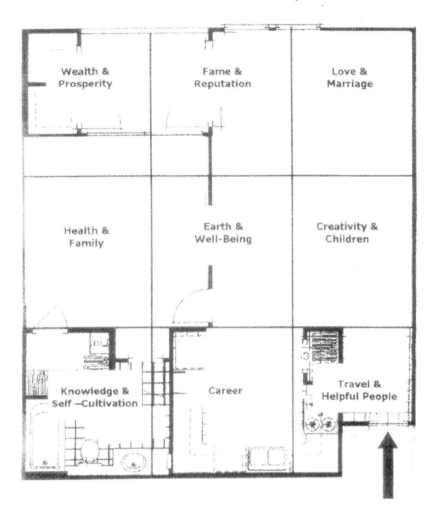

Your front entrance is the position or standpoint for determining the orientation of the Bagua map. The front entrance is the front of the Bagua Map. Once you've determined which Bagua area your front door is in, the rest of the areas can be easily located.

Remember whatever the shape of your home is fit it completely inside the Bagua map so that the entire structure is within the nine sections of the map. If the building is square, rectangular, the Bagua map is stretched to accommodate the structure of the home. If the home is the shape of an L, T, S, or U, there will be Bagua areas on the map that will be outside the structure of the home. Here are some examples.

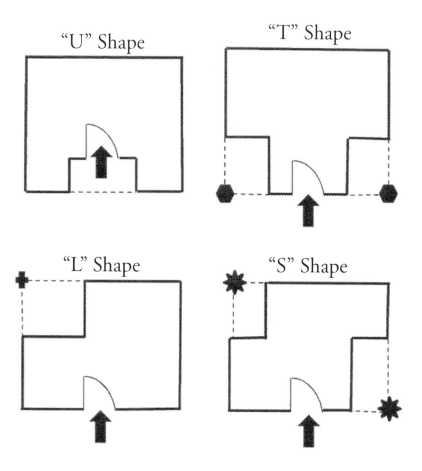

"U" Shape

"T" Shape

"L" Shape

"S" Shape

It is important that there are no missing areas in the Bagua. When this happens and there are missing areas on your map you can take care of this problem by lining up the outer walls of your structure. Where the two lines meet and intersect complete your Bagua with a plant, tree, fountain, or by burying a mineral. If the area is cemented you can paint a symbol on the service symbolizing the two points meeting or if possible place a potted plant there. You want to do this for there should be no areas missing.

The Bagua map divides the floor plan into nine areas. Each of the areas is called areas of the Bagua map or Life areas. Each area holds a different energy and corresponds to a specific area of your life. If your home is square the sizes of these areas are equal. If you have an odd shaped house or structure the sizes of the area will vary. The actual size of the different areas is not as important and does not influence your life as much as the energy contained in these areas. The Bagua map enables you to pinpoint the areas you need to work on and then to proceed with knowledge and awareness of what you would like to change or manifest.

For example, if you want to improve your love life you would go to the marriage partnership area of the Bagua. Remember it correlates to the structure of your home so it is the furthest right back area from your front entrance. Enhance the area of each room of the home besides the main area when you want HUGE changes in your love life.

The map also correlates to the floor plan and structure were you work. Your office, cubicle, desk etc....it is a good idea always to Feng Shui wherever you are spending your time and energy. Feng Shui your hotel room when you travel to make you feel at home. Bring a small picture, a colorful scarf, and fresh flowers into the space. It takes about five minutes and voila, it's your space. Make a little map of the Bagua so when you travel you can hold it while you are standing at the entrance of the room you are staying in. This will help you figure out the placement of the room. After a while with enough practice you won't need the map. You will just know.

Here is the Bagua Map with the colors, elements and attributes associated with the life areas.

ABUNDANCE & PROSPERITY Purples, reds, and blues "Gratitude"	ILLUMINATION FAME & REPUTATION Reds "Integrity"	LOVE & REPUTATION Whites, pinks, and reds "Receptivity"
FOUNDATION & FAMILY Blues, and greens "Strength"	HEALTH & WELL BEING Yellow and earth tones "Earth"	CREATIVITY & CHILDREN White and pastels "Joy"
SKILL & INNER KNOWLEDGE Black, blues and greens "Stillness"	CAREER & LIFE'S JOURNEY Black and dark tones "Depth"	HELPFUL PEOPLE & Travel White, grey, and black "Synchronicity"

∧   ∧   ∧

FRONT ENTRANCE

The nine Life Areas of the Bagua Map and their corresponding locations, colors and elements are as follows:

1. HEALTH: Located in the center of the map. Colors: Yellow and Earth Tones- Element: Earth

2. HELPFUL PEOPLE AND TRAVEL: Located in the right front area of the space. Colors: Gray, White and Black- Element: Metal

3. CAREER: Located in the center front. Colors: Black and Midnight Blue- Element: Water

4. KNOWLEDGE AND INNER SKILL: Located in the front left. Colors Blue, Green, Black- Element: Mountain Earth

5. HEALTH AND FAMILY: Located in the center left Colors: Green and Blue- Element: Wood

6. WEALTH AND PROSPERITY: Located in the back left Colors: Purple, Reds, Blues- Element: Fire

7. FAME AND REPUTATION: Located in the back center Color: Red Element: Fire

8. MARRIAGE AND PARTNERSHIP: Located in the back right Colors: Red, Pink, and White- Receptive Earth

9. CHILDREN AND CREATIVITY: Located in the center right Colors: White and Pastels- Element Metal

See If You Know the Feng Shui Answers

Feng Shui (pronounced Fung Shway)

A Chinese term meaning "wind + water" practiced for over Three Thousand Years

Feng Shui literally means wind and water. It is rapidly becoming a universal practice for creating the perfect environment in which to live and work.

Elements

Metal   Wood   Water   Fire   Earth

What: The Chinese art of _____

There is a Chinese saying……..."If you want change in your life, move 27 things in your house".

There are three basic principles that form the foundation on which Feng Shui is built.

These principles define _____ (energy around us)

Everything is _____

Everything is _____

Everything is _____

When: When to apply principles

Increase your _____

Enhance your _____

Boost your _____

Upgrade your _____, in any way

Where:

_____   _____

_____   _____

How: Balance the _____ _____

Mixing the five elements _____   _____

_____   _____   _____

Locating your treasures – How to use the _____

Bagua_____ Bagua _____

Why: To bring people back into healthful _____

*Answers are in the back pages of the book

The Archangel for Feng Shui and Interior Designers is Archangel Jophiel. For many reasons Archangel Jophiel is one of my favorite angels. When I call upon her sometimes I feel or sense her presence when I am doing my Feng Shui classes. I feel her gentle guidance for what the class needs to hear. When I have a de-cluttering job to do for a client and I feel overwhelmed, I call upon her for help.

She works magic. Call upon her if you are having problems with the de-cluttering or designing your space. She will help you get rid of the clutter and clear the energy around you. All you have to do is ask. It is that simple. Ask her to be your own Spiritual Interior designer and Spiritual Feng Shui consultant.

When we tap into our higher self we realize we are really spirits living in a human form. It is a natural process communicating with angels we just have forgotten. Angels are the messengers from heaven. To work with angels is to have all the help you need for making your life the most fruitful. Why not ask for their help? As they, say nothing to lose but everything to gain.

Meditation to Feng Shui Your Home

Calling in your higher self-sit upright, back straight; toes pointed a little in to align your spinal column with your inner tube of light that sits right in front of it. Imagine this inner tube of light connected to your spinal column from the top of your head to bottom of your spinal column. Close your eyes, take three deep breaths one…….. Two…….. three ……… relax your feet, your ankles, your calves, your knees, your thighs, and your buttocks area. Relax your body up through your trunk, arms, fingers, neck, and head.

Now there is an abundance of golden white light energy coming down from heaven. …..From the top of your head breathe in all the golden white light energy from source…… breath out any negativity…….. Breath in all the golden white light energy…….. breath out any negativity,……..breath in all the golden white light energy……… breath out all negativity……….. You become filled with the golden white light energy and you start breathing it in and breathing it out….. Now begin to visualize an Angel in the distant coming towards you. It is Archangel Jophiel. You call out her name three times.

Jophiel, Jophiel, Jophiel, she gently takes your hand and you are both standing in front of your home. You can clearly, sense, feel, and see it. This is where your desires and dreams are created. You can feel the energy coming from your home. How does it feel? What is it saying to you? How does the face of your home look? What would you change if you could?

You and Jophiel decide to go inside the home. How does it feel? Does it feel warm and inviting? Do you feel loved and appreciated? If not, what would you change to make you feel at home? Take a look around in the room you are standing in. Does this room express who you are? Does it express who you want to be? If not, what are the changes you will make here in this space? Feel the newly made changes coming from your heart.

Take your time and when you feel complete leave the space and travel into the space in your home that is your favorite. What special qualities does this space have that you would like to incorporate in the other areas of your home? Consult with Archangel Jophiel on how you would go about doing this. What would you change to bring in your heart's desire?

Take some time to embellish in every space in your home.

Know that these spaces literally express who you are and what you become in life. Start to feel energized, happy, and elated at all the new possibilities.........

Jophiel takes your hand and you are back at the front entrance of your home. You turn and sense the life and breathe of your home. In however way you wish express gratitude to your home. You see the life you breathe into your home and it in return will breaths life in you. As you say goodbye to your home you also say goodbye to Jophiel. Know that you can return at any time to this space and that Jophiel will be there as your own Spiritual Interior Designer to assist you with your home.

Allow yourself now to return, let your breath be the pathway for bringing you back. You are now coming back feeling relaxed, inspirited and energized. Breathing in and breathing out......Coming fully back now......Open your eyes....You are back and ready for all the Blessings that are manifesting.........

The Center

Now that you have completed the task of drawing your floor plan and overlaying the Bagua map over it as shown in chapter one, we are ready to begin on working on the individual areas. We are going to start with the center of your home or living space, which is the center of the Bagua Map. This is the area of the map that I find key to your life because the center represents you. You are the center that everything in your life revolves around.

The element related to this area is Earth. The element of Earth gives us a solid base and magnifies the importance of being grounded. We need to do this to function properly on this Earth plane. It is important to cultivate a sense of being grounded and centered within ourselves.

Because it is so important for us to be grounded and centered it is a good practice to start every morning when you wake up with some grounding exercises. This could be as simple as visualizing, sensing, or feeling the bottoms of your feet having roots growing out of them and going down deep into Mother Earth. Once this is established you connect yourself with the magnetic power of the earth, the basis and foundation of all our support. Imagine that you are fully in your body and feel that grounding and balancing. Stay there until you feel your body shift into a well-grounded state. Doing simple exercises like this will support you to create the strong foundation you need to begin the work for your transformation.

Your whole life revolves around you. You are the creator of your destiny. Because your destiny is determined by the choices you make in your life, choose wisely. Call upon your higher self and become aware of when you are sabotaging yourself. Observe your thoughts from your higher self. Are your thoughts the truth of who you really are or are they just stories?

We are starting from the center of the Bagua map so you will be able to create life improvements in all areas of your life. The center impacts all the areas in the Bagua just as the center of a wheel that radiates out. For this reason this is the area to begin and re-script your life. This area also represents your health. Your health and vitality are crucial for you achieving your fullest potential. If your health suffers every part of your life suffers. Here being in balance is very important to keep you healthy. You want to balance the feminine and masculine, the Yin and the Yang parts of you.

The Light and the Dark, The Feminine and the Masculine, The Yin and the Yang.

We are going to look at your physical environment. The physical environment is where you live or work. Take a look at the center of your home or workplace. Ideally the center should be open, airy, and free. The center should be healthy, bright and uplifting. If it is cluttered you will have a cluttered mind. You will fill 'stuck'. It is like burying yourself alive physically and spiritually. I see people walking around physically but they are lifeless. Because they live in a cluttered enviroment they have buried their treasures, their passions, their gifts, and their very essence.

When I ask you to de-clutter I am not only talking about clutter on the surfaces, I am also talking about clutter in drawers and shelves. In Feng Shui there is no place to hide. You can physically get sick when things are not in order and are cluttered around you, especially in the center of your home.

This area should be a place of peace. I recently went on a house call to Feng Shui and de-clutter a client's home. The next morning I had a phone call from the client telling me she had a good night's sleep for the first time in a long time. That same week I had another client telling me after we de-cluttered, it lifted him out of his depression and he felt like he could start living again.

If there is excess in this area, get rid of the excess because it will be impossible to keep this area in order. That is why they call it excess.

Also take a look at the lighting in your home. Is there enough sufficient natural light or do you need to add more light. This is especially important for adequate lighting is essential for creating an uplifting feeling. Is there any part of this area that is dark, gloomy, or unwelcoming? You can increase the natural lighting by adding full spectrum light bulbs. The colors in this area need to be attractive to you. They need to invigorate you and make you feel alive. Live the colors you love or you'll never feel completely at home in your own space.

The color of health in this area is the color yellow, the color of the sun. If you like this color paints your walls in this area the shades of yellow or gold. Yellow is also the color of your solar plexus, the color of self-empowerment. Let the sunshine start coming in…………colors in your outside environment affect you internally. If painting the walls yellow in this area is not an option, place square or rectangular yellow objects in the center of your home. Be creative. This area which is the element of Earth is symbolized by the shape of the square or rectangle. Look at the Chinese coin. It is a circle with a square in the center, symbolizing good fortune.

Check out your possessions in this area. Everything you own and possess has something to say about you. Look at this space from your higher self. Is this area of your home saying nice things to you? See if the things you have in this space deplete your energy or give you energy. Do they represent sad times, a broken heart, or a feeling of lacking. Make sure the things you have in this space have only nice things to say.

Release anything that pulls your energy in a negative way. For example, if you have a painting or a picture that upsets you every time you look at it, get rid of it. You don't have to understand why but it is important to honor your feelings. Listen to your gut feelings that are speaking loudly to you. Get rid of things that pull your energy down. If you don't listen to your inner voice you will become off balance and feel off centered.

One Feng Shui house call that was a strong example of energy pulling in a negative way was of a client who was unaware of what she was doing to herself every day. When I entered her home my eye went to this beautiful oil painting of her. It was in the center of her home. I let her know how beautiful I thought the painting of her was. Her eyes started to water.

She proceeded to tell me the story of her ex-husband and how he had cheated on her at the time when he had the oil painting done. Needless to say every time she looked at the painting, it reminded her of that and made her painfully sad. We immediately took down the painting. It was sucking her energy. Without her realizing it by having the painting on the wall she kept repeating the sad story. After taking the picture down she felt a dark cloud lift off of her. She felt and was empowered to create a new story.

Another Feng Shui job I was encountered with something that felt evil. I was called to Feng Shui a home to get rid of the bad luck that a family of four were having. When I arrived at the home I stood at the front entrance. In the center of the home was a piano. I immediately had a bad feeling about the piano and inquired about it. They told me that the piano was a rental that they'd had for about six months, the same amount of time that they had with the bad luck. The husband played the piano and soon after broke his hand. They had hired two different piano teachers for their two daughters, the first teacher they hired would always holler at the children making them cry. The other teacher scribbled all over their children's sheet music.

When I looked at the sheet music with the scribbling it was unreadable and it was crazy looking. Their two daughters never learned how to play the piano. I told them to get rid of the piano immediately. They did and they called me a week later after they got rid of the piano and everything in their lives began to get better. The important message here was for them to always listen to their inner voice and to honor and follow their own true feelings.

Even though sometimes we can't see energy it does not mean that it does not exist. All energy is real. We are a solid mass of energy that we can see and there is more energy around us that we don't see. So if you feel something even though you cannot see it, your higher self and inner wisdom will speak to you both physically and emotionally. Start listening to it and follow your true feelings.

Bringing you back to the center, look at this space and see if it is enhanced with art works that hold meaning to you. Does the art make your heart sing? Remember this area represents you so make it beautiful, whimsical colorful, peaceful, or dramatic. Make it your expression. Bring in an object or piece of art that reminds you to stay centered in all your activities. The rule of thumb is to surround yourself only with items you love.

Do you feel peaceful when you are in this space? If you don't, what do you need to change? Listen to your inner voice and trust what you are hearing, feeling, or sensing. This is your opportunity to make changes. Remember you are the center of your world that you and you alone create.

Does this space please your sense of smell? This is very important for your sense of smell triggers memories, it can heighten your sense of awareness, your sense of sensuality, and it can make you feel loved. If there is a bad smell take care of it immediately or you will eventually become numb to it and it will affect your health. I have gone to homes with bad smells and the clients were desensitized to it. Take care of it ASAP and replace with aromatic deliciously scented candles or potpourri. Put in some fresh citrus, sensuous vanilla or any fragrance you especially enjoy. This will give your sense of wellbeing and health a boost

Bring in vital healthy energy and bring in some plants. Placing fresh, healthy green plants in the center of your home is a great life cure. An odd number of plants like three, five, or seven can create more activity and change for health.

More uplifting cures for this area are crystals which also represents the Earth element. One of my favorite crystals is yellow golden citrine. It is one of the two minerals on the planet which does not hold and accumulate any negative energy but dissipates and transmutes it. It activates and opens your solar plexus and nourishes and balances your physical, emotional, spiritual and mental bodies. How wonderful is that.

The inner works that I recommend for you to do are exercises and meditations that ground and center you. If possible during the day take yourself out physically and be in the sun. Stand in the grass and allow yourself to feel your being. Light researchers indicate that the body intrinsically needs to consume natural light on a daily basis. Imagine and feel the light of the sun going in your body and healing you on a DNA level. Play with it. The mind and what you think is very powerful. Call in your higher self to observe and visualize and picture the golden white light energy of the sun emerging you in its energy. Bring in that energy to heal every part of your being.

The sun's light will activate, energize and balance your system. The bands of natural sunlight are composed of the colors of the rainbow which correlate to the energy centers (chakra centers) in the body. Each Chakra center radiates a different color. The chakra centers are energy centers that run in a vertical line along your spinal column.

The color red is at the base of your spin, the color orange is under you belly button, the color yellow is at your solarplex, the color green is at your heart, the color blue is at your throat, the color indigo is at your third eye, the color violet/white is at your crown, the top of the head. These energy centers in the body are your natural connection to the divine light. Fill yourself up with light. The human body was designed to absorb and assimilate rainbow energy through sunlight. Do this inner work with sufficient sunlight and you will feel happy and alive.

Sunlight also produces serotonin which is a chemical involved in the brains electric transmissions that regulates mood, appetite and energy levels. If you need to eat healthier sitting in the sun will help you with your diet. If you feel sad sitting in the sun will put a smile on your face. If you feel tired take a delicious 20 minute sun bath and see how it energizes you. Try to make this a practice and you will see subtle changes that will eventually turn into big changes. Take time to journal at least 15 minutes every morning. Write down how you would like to improve your health and life. What changes you are willing to make. Or what changes are you willing to do to keep you healthy, happy, and with inner peace. Write a contract to yourself and honor it. Examples would be: I will do yoga three times a week. I will exercise and eat less sugar. I will take time out during the day to meditate or journal. I will keep only good thoughts in my head and digest and release out the rest.

Besides writing down how you would improve your health, write down what areas of your life that you would like to change to feel more centered. What relationships would you like to improve upon? How would you like to change the relationship to yourself to feel more centered and at peace? Think about it, take your time, and be gentle with yourself. Make your new mantra: I experience life easily, effortlessly, and joyfully, and my being is filled with peace. I work with my higher self and I am blissful.

Inner work that is very helpful that I recommend is to also practice breathing. Yes, breathing. Breath is our life force and most of us are always holding our breath. Start breathing from the bottom of your stomach and fill it up. Most of us do shallow breathing from our chest which is so wrong for our optimum health.

There is a technique called Pranic breathing which has long been used by yogis as a way of energizing energy centers that run through the body. Prana is life force energy. When you work with this breathing system it will facilitate to release old belief systems and old patterns of behavior that need clearing. The old no longer needed pattern of behavior is released and cleansed from the entire body. After practicing breathing this way I feel more balanced and energized. If this is something that feels right to you I highly recommend looking up Prana Breath meditation.

The last thing I recommend for Inner work is to incorporate something fun in your schedule every week that will make you feel balanced and whole again. It could be dancing, singing, taking an art class, walking in nature or by the beach, or flying a kite. I sing in the choir. When I sing I feel so connected and whole. It transports me to a place of being. Start having fun and bring in something that fills your heart and lets your spirit soar. This will bring you the inner peace and balance that might be missing.

I know I have given you a lot of "to do's" with both outer work and inner work. Please be patient and gentle with yourselves. Do those things that are the ones nagging you the most. It takes more energy just thinking about what we want to do than just doing it. At the end of this book there are charts that will help you prioritize and get organized. Good Luck.

The Angels to Assist This Area

Archangel Raphael is the Archangel for health and wellbeing. Raphael is heaven's angel of healing. I call upon him when I need to eat healthy. I love my sweets. I call upon him when I am putting off exercise which

I know is for my optimal health. I especially call upon him when I am stressed.

Often when I am stressed I hold my breath unconsciously. We need to breathe for oxygenating our mind, body and spirit. Have him help you take deep breaths and to exhale slowly to awaken your energy and to releases old patterns. Use his green energy ray of healing when you are sick. Visualize his green healing light and having it enter every cell of your body, circulating and healing you and dissolving the bonds of negative pattern atoms. Visualize or feel this healing light cover your whole body dissolving all bonds to fear-based thought patterns. You will feel freer and lighter bringing in health. Also give your cares and worries to Him. I tell my students to visualize a big bucket in front of them and to put all their worries in the bucket. Give Raphael the bucket. Release and let go. Ask Raphael to surround anyone needing healing that you are aware of with his emerald green aura. I use this technique with my clients, friends and family. A long time ago my mom was feeling worried and I gave her this technique before she went to sleep. She was able to fall asleep and it made her feel better. The crystals that are aligned with Raphael's healing energy are emeralds and malachite.

For Rainbow energy and sun energy call upon Archangel Razial, he is the Rainbow Archangel. He is also known as the 'wizard Archangel' because he is 'wise and magical'. His name means "Secret of God". If you want to heal blockages as well as imbalances that are causing negative patterns visualize rainbow-colored light around yourself or someone else. He will help you with your everyday thinking and align you with your true essence. You will feel his healing magic in a rainbow crystal. In the morning when you wake up call upon him and imagine yourself wrapped in sheets of rainbow light.

Archangel Haniel helps you with sensitivity and when you are emotionally upset. When you are extra-sensitive she will help you in embracing and accepting all parts of yourself. She will help you appreciate yourself and show you how your sensitivity is a gift. Being sensitive helps you to tune into the truth about people and situations. With Haniel her gentleness she will help you trust that inner voice that protects you. Call upon her and she will help you distinguish between your own feelings and those feelings you are picking up from others. Her comfort will support and help you. She will help bring back your inner peace and balance. Use her pink healing ray to feel compassion and love for yourself and others. I sometimes ask her to place a Hugh pink mirror behind me so that when I am communicating with another in a difficult situation my words are reflecting back to them with love. The crystal rose quartz will help you tap into her energy.

Powers are angels of physical healing. They are Hugh angels and can embrace you with their majestic energy field. Their large angel wings are tipped with a greenish white glow for healing. Allow yourself with your higher self to be embraced by their wings and feel the healing.

Angelic Healing Meditation with the Powers

Sit upright, back straight; toes pointed a little in to align your spinal column with your inner tube of light that sits right in front of it. Imagine the inner tube of light connected to your spinal column from the top of your head to bottom of your spinal column. Close your eyes, take three deep breaths: one......two.......three...... relax your feet, your ankles, your calves, your knees, your thighs, and your buttocks area. Relax your body up through your trunk, arms, fingers, neck, and head. Now imagine there is an abundance of golden white light energy coming down from heaven. Breathe in all the golden white light energy from source and breath out and release any negativity, again breath in all the golden white light energy, and once again breath in all the golden white light energy. You become filled with the golden white light energy and you start breathing it in and breathing it out. Now begin to visualize angels in the distant coming towards you. They are tall and beautiful. They give off a pearlescent glow and their wings are outstretched. You see them as they come closer. Their wing tips are a greenish white. These angels are called Powers. You call them closer by calling out their names three times. Powers, powers, powers, we call upon you who have healing as your primary function. Please surround me with your wings. You can feel their enormous wings give off an electrical or magnetic emanation that goes directly in your body and acts as a healing force...... you participate with them........together with them you are programming your mind to heal, you are programing to eat the proper foods, and you are programing to get enough rest.........you stay there for a while soaking in all the healing energy. You are changing and healing on a deep cellular level.....you feel the angel's warmth, their love and light and you are receptive to the gifts of healing. They absorb any illness, pain or negativity you have been holding on to and that you are ready to release. You stay there allowing the grace and the breath of this moment to be absorbed into your soul.

You begin to bring yourself up, breathing deeply. Before you come all the way up to consciousness, you ask the Powers to stay or come whenever you need them. You know you only have to say their name three times and they will be there. Now bring yourself all the way up. On the count of three you will be back one…. Coming back….two opening your eyes…..three you are back…..feeling marvelous.

Helpful People and Travel

The next area of your life we are going to work on is Helpful people and travel. This area is located at the bottom right hand corner of the Bagua map.

This area is designated for the helpful people in your life and it is the area to put out the intention to bring in more helpful people. It is also the area you put out the intentions of the places to which you would love to travel. I will give examples in this chapter on how you can go about doing this. Where intention goes manifestation flows.

The Chinese believe that there are three realms of influence in your life: Heaven, Earth, and Human. To get the most out of your life circumstances, you need positive conditions in each of these realms. According to Chinese belief, aligning your life, your activities and thought, with the natural order of all three realms, brings you good luck and success. This area of the Bagua will influence these three realms.

The Heaven realm is where miracles and other unexpected interventions happen. In this area of the Bagua put the intention there to have the heavens open and to have heaven's luck. You can put out the intention that you have the support of a heavenly crew. This can be metaphorically or physically.

The Earth realm provides humans with all the materials needed to sustain life such as food, shelter, and clothing. How you position and orient yourself in life and in your surroundings enormously impacts your welfare and destiny. Working with Feng Shui you are working with the Earth luck. To obtain all our earthly material needs we cannot do it alone we need helpful people.

The Human realm addresses the need to have the right people around you. This will create success in your projects and will bless you with Human luck. This area calls in success and the helpful people needed for that success. I will give you examples on the following pages on how to call them in.

Using this area of your life to its fullest potential allows you to wake up to the power and influence of Feng Shui. With this knowledge you have a chance to increase your success and grow into your fullest potential.

The element for helpful people and travel is metal. Metal activates and amplifies this area. The colors for this area are white, grey, and black.

You address this area of helpful people and travel when you want to:

1. Sell your home or move to a new home

2. Attract more helpful people, clients, friends, or mentors, in your life.

3. Be connected more spiritually to the being or beings that you ask to guide you: "helpful people"

4. Travel or go to a specific place.

When you want to move or sell your home there are different solutions. I am going to share some stories and experiences in Feng Shui for this purpose.

Years ago my sister Maria wanted to sell her home. I called her to help Feng Shui her home but her husband Jim was home instead. As a Feng Shui master I instructed him on what to do. The area of helpful people and travel was in their garage so I had him place a piece of paper in foil in the front right hand corner of the garage. On the paper he wrote down that he had more buyers than he could imagine, that they sold their home fast, and that they received more money than what they were asking. Later that day my sister came home at noon to meet with the real estate person and sign papers for selling the house. Well before my sister could sign the papers, there was a knock at the door. Someone found out that she was selling her home, wanted to buy it and the cost didn't matter. The realtor heard this and told my sister she would take less commission if she would still work with her. Needless to say, there were other offers on the house even before the sign was in the front yard and the home was sold by midnight that evening.

My sister had no idea what had just happened. Her husband and I told her what we had done. We also told her we fixed the wealth corner and wrote out a check for the amount they wanted with the saying "this or something better". I always tell clients to put this or something better for the highest good of all concerned and it always turns out better than expected.

A few years ago I was asked to go look at a home in Palm Springs that had been on the market for a long time. For some reason they had difficulty in selling it. As I approached the outside front of the home I thought why wasn't anyone attracted to this beautiful place. When I went inside my question was answered immediately. I felt death and stuffiness in the air as I stood in the front entrance. The air felt heavy. I went into helpful people and travel area of the home and there were pictures of dead actors who had committed suicide. There was also a broken window in the room. We made the necessary changes in this area such as taking down the pictures and fixing the window. We fixed other areas of the home, moved things around. After we made the necessary changes within two weeks the first person that walked through the property bought the home. Whether you are selling your home or looking at what you have in this area of your home, make sure it feels right.

Real estate agents often use Feng Shui to sell homes. After "staging" the property we always take a look at helpful people and travel. We make a list of the helpful people to sell the home and we write down that we have many clients that love the home and will buy the home easily, effortlessly, and joyfully. Putting this intention out creates a demand for the property and often because of the competition they will pay over the selling price to get the property.

Another time I had a client who wanted the buyers who purchased the home to love it. So that was the affirmation we wrote down for him and he got buyers who loved the home. The affirmations are written on a piece of paper and put in a metal box or foil. Metal is used because the element for this area is metal. It is placed in the bottom right hand front corner of the room from the room entrance. I have been practicing Feng Shui since 1985 and this has always worked. Like my first teacher in Feng Shui told me, if something works why not do it.

When you want to bring in helpful people of any kind to support you, write down their names or imagine the perfect person coming to help you. I once had a student that had shared with me that one of her heart's desires was to win a landscaping contest that was being held by a prestigious landscape business in our area. She didn't think to enter because she said she didn't believe she had a chance. I told her to go for it and do some Feng Shui remedies. She wrote down all the helpful people that would help her win this contest. She worked on her garden. Put the amount of money that she would win on a check and placed it in her wealth corner and voilà! She e-mailed me a few weeks later with a newspaper article. The newspaper had her garden on the front page of the home and gardens section. She won…. she was shocked and happy!

The area of helpful people and travel also works hand in hand with the wealth and prosperity corner. This happens because both areas are diagonally across from one another.

Would you like to travel or go to a specific place? This is the area to address if you love to travel. A couple of years ago I wanted to go back to Europe with my husband Marshall so I placed a picture of us at the

International airport terminal on his desk in the helpful people and travel area. In two weeks he came home and wanted to know if I wanted to go to Spain. Of course I said, "Yes'. This could be a coincidence but last year in June after putting a few Irish paraphernalia out we went to Ireland. Try it out and see how powerful pictures, intentions, affirmations can be when placed in the right places. Where would you like to go and visit? Put a picture up and visualize you in it.

The Angels to Call Upon for This Area

An Archangel to call upon for crystal clear intentions and taking a trip is Archangel Michael. He will help you to be bold to admit what you truly desire and focus on it with unwavering faith. For this thought to work you must feel that you deserve the best of everything, in all ways. Michael's aura is royal blue mixed with tinges of royal purple. He will protect you on where ever you are as he is God's main man when it comes to protecting and defending. The crystal stone associated with archangel Michael is sugalite.

Your guardian angel is the perfect angel for helpful people and travel. Who better than your guardian angel to call upon. They are sent by God to give us protection and guidance. Have you ever hear a little voice inside you guiding you when you need help or when you instantly become aware of being in harm's way? That is your guardian angel. They can communicate with us telepathically. They can't interfere with our lives because we have free will but if we ask for their help they are right there for us. We can even ask them to go and talk to another person's guardian angel on our behalf when we find it difficult to communicate with that person. They give unconditional love and light. How blessed we are to have them as a friend.

Archangel Chamuel is an angel to call upon when you have a hard time visualizing or seeing things how they really are. He is an Archangel that is sees everything. His name means "God sees". He sees everything. Call upon Chamuel to find things. Big or small, he can even help you find yourself…..you're true self….Feng Shui is all about becoming aware of what you're unaware of and he can help you with that. Chamuel also engenders peacefulness. Ask him to help you with personal inner peace, peace within relationships or situations, and world peace. Chamuel's aura is pale green and he is associated with green fluorite crystal.

The Archangel that is helpful when you experience loss is Archangel Azriel. He helps you with your loved ones to make the transition to heaven at the time of their physical death. He surrounds the newly crossed–over soul with loving light to make the experience uplifting and comforting. Azriel was so helpful and comforting to me when my husband's mother died. I prayed that he would help her passing because I knew she was afraid. I asked him for a sign that he heard my prayers. I spoke with the nurse the morning she died. She told me how happy my mother-in-law was the day before she died. That morning she died with a smile on her face. That was my sign. I knew Archangel Azriel was with her.

A Meditation for Contacting Your Angel

Sit or lie in a comfortable, meditative position. Close your eyes. Relax your feet, your ankles, your calves, your knees, your thighs, and your buttocks area. Relax your body up through your trunk, arms, fingers, neck, and head.

Now there is an abundance of golden white light energy and it is coming down from the heavens. It is surrounding you going faster and faster. It goes around the room you are in. It goes in and around the surrounding rooms. It goes around the building faster and faster and goes back up to the heavens. Take three deep breaths......one........two......three........ now transport yourself mentally to an open field of green grass. Imagine that within this open field of green grass you are standing on a path that stretches off into the distance.

You are with your higher self and you start to walk up the path, and as you do, you see in the distance a form coming toward you.............. This form is radiating a clear, bright, iridescent white light.

As the form approaches, you begin to feel it, sense it......... Let the love of God from this angel envelop you. The closer this form gets the more details you can see of the face and appearance.

Greet this angel and ask what his or her name is. Take whatever name comes to you first and don't worry about it.

Ask your angel if there is anything he or she would like to say to you or advice he or she would like to give you at the moment. If you wish you can ask some specific questions.....

You may get immediate answers but, if not, don't be discouraged….the answers will come to you in some form later.

When the experience of being together feels complete, thank your angel, express your appreciation, and ask him or her to meet you again. Say goodbye then with three deep breaths, bring yourself back up from your feet to your head. One, breathe and feel your breath, two, bring yourself back up three, you are back in your body feeling truly blessed that you have such a friend.

Career

Your career area is located in the center front of the structure you are working with. It is between skill and inner knowledge, helpful people and travel.

The element that is represented here and to place here is water. This is an element we cannot live without. This element keeps us in the flow of life and gives us the gift of self-reflection.

In the career area everyone strives for their life purpose. This is the area to work on to make your career better or to change your career. There are five paths in your life to choose from. You have two lower paths, a middle path, and two higher paths. It is up to you to choose the path you want to journey on. Why not choose your highest path.

To get to this highest path we start with the inner work. Start to meditate. Meditation begins the empowering journey of self-realization. It helps you dive into the watery world of feelings to seek your truth. Meditate and develop your self-reflective skills so that you may come to know yourself in an intimate way. Meditate and examine yourself with an open heart and wise eye to see what you wish to improve and how you want to change. If you get stuck in the process, it may be a sign you are too hard or critical. That is your inner covert critic child. Place the inner covert critic child in the corner while you work with your higher self. When you choose to blame others and are constantly pointing a finger at life's situations instead of claiming responsibility for your own actions, this shows that you need to muster up the courage to face the enemy within. Let go of the illusions and be willing to dive into the watery depths of your own feelings and discover the role of your spiritual essence. Observing yourself from your higher self will help you to do this. Your essence calls you to delve deeper, to know yourself, and to trust your path. Start meditating so that you may get a new balanced sense of self. You will have this new sense to embrace its potential again and again. To "follow our bliss" can be one of the greatest challenges of our lives. But by meditating and connecting with our higher self and plumbing our own debts we are able to find the answers to our career questions and emerge buoyant and ready to focus our energies on our new career goals.

A tool that works hand in hand with this is intention. When you have a strong intention to create something it is very likely to manifest in your life. There are three elements from within which make up intention. # 1. Desire…You must have a true desire to have. Do you truly in your heart, desire this goal to be realized? #2. Belief… The more you believe in your desire and the possibility of attaining it, the more certain you will do so. You have to believe. And then #3 Receive… You must be willing to receive and have that which you are seeking. Many times we want blessings in our lives and are not willing to receive because a little voice inside says "No, no, I am not worthy". We stop the process because we do not allow ourselves to receive. Listen to see if you are doing this and change this little voice to a different mantra. Create a little voice that says "I am worthy to receive".

Intention is the sum total of the parts: desire, belief, and receiving. To create intention you have to have all three parts. The clearer and stronger your intention, with a strong desire and belief the more quickly and easily your goals will manifest. I always tell my students to put their intentions out there and add the phrase "this or something better". Sometimes we get what we want and when we get it we say what was I thinking? So if we add the phrase "this or something better" it always turns out better than we can ever imagine. The universe has a way of always knowing what is best for us and what is for our highest good. The key is to have the ego let go of control, put it in the corner of the room, and let it know that it is safe while you work with spirit. When you work with your higher self and do this process and start to work with spirit, it will create a healthier ego and will allow the process of manifestation to come to fruition.

Now that you know about the inner work for this area I would like to discuss your physical environment. Because the career area is the center front of the Bagua it is often times the entrance of our home. Make your front entrance full of light. A dark entrance implies a dark future, a difficult career, and difficulty in making money. The ideal entrance creates bright and positive feelings.

If there is not enough natural lighting add proper lighting to your front entrance inside and out. Adding light is an easy and effective way to up the energy of your entrance and it is lighting the way for wealth to find your door. Another Feng Shui enhancement is to flank the front entrance with greeters. Greeters can be represented by two beautiful pots of flowers or flank two luscious green succulent plants on either side of the door. Placing succulent plants at the entrance of a home symbolizes money coming in. Also, placing succulents on either side of all the entrances to the home will emphasize the flow of money.

I recently had a real state client who was experiencing a down ward turn in his career. The first thing I noticed approaching his home was that all the lighting on the pathway leading to his front entrance was out. He also had overgrown foliage that was blocking the path making it difficult to get to the front door. When I got to the front door it was hard to open. The knob was not working. I told him what he had to fix was the lighting on the path way immediately. Adding light was crucial for lighting the way for wealth to find his door. This would also up the energy of his entrance and light the way for people to find his door. He needed to cut down the overgrown foliage that was blocking the pathway. He was also blocking the pathway to his clients, friends and family. He needed to fix the front door that was stuck. A door that is stuck symbolically represents not allowing new opportunities to come in. Within a week I heard from him and he had fixed all the problems. He was so excited about the turn of events after he did the Feng Shui cures that he wanted to refer all his friends to me. In life sometimes we are unaware of what we are unaware of and Feng Shui just points things out to how we self-sabotage ourselves.

Because of the position of the career area on the bagua map being the front center it most often is where the front door of the home is. The front door in Feng Shui is the mouth of the home. It is the main entrance for vital energy coming in the home and is the place of first impressions. Make sure your front door is a representation of the first impression you want to make. Does it need to be painted, fixed, and have a full range of motion or does it have clutter behind it or is it blocked in any way? Doors represent opportunities in our life. When the door of opportunity arrives do you take the opportunity? Do you shut the door on new possibilities or on people in your life? Do you have a full range of motion in your decisions in life? Doors represent our ability to make intelligent clear decisions. Tap into your own inner wisdom, look at your front door, allow vital energy to come into the home, and create that great first impression that truly represents you.

The career area has the water element. In Feng Shui the water signifies your wealth and flowing water creates your cash flow. Water features in this area of your home such as fountains, waterfalls, and aquariums are ideal for this area. Always make sure the water is flowing into the home towards the home not away from it. This symbolizes money flowing in your home. If the water is flowing away from the home it symbolizes money flowing out so you want water to always flow towards the home.

A little ritual I perform in the morning is to go down stairs and turn the fountain on. It symbolizes to me all the abundance flowing in and my gratitude for this. All during the day I hear the water and it very soothing and healing. Also representing the water element and great for front entrances are mirrors, crystals, and the colors black and deep blues or art depicting bodies of water.

Take a look at the career area when you are seeking a purpose in life, when you want to make a career change, or when you want to be more courageous. In this area place any image that personally symbolizes your career. Put in quotes, sayings, and affirmations related to courage following one's path in life. Fix hard edges and put in some lush green healthy plants symbolizing your lush, green, healthy path. This area concerns your work, career success, and how you make a living.

If you want to find a better job, get a promotion, develop better relationships with your co-workers, or receive recognition for your work, this is the place to take a good look at. Because the career area is in front of the home, this area is also connected to your relationship with the world outside of your home. And what is a career, if not a relationship to the outer world.

Make sure this area is de-cluttered. Get rid of the roadblocks in your life. One of my students removed twenty-seven items out of her entryway when I told the class about a Chinese saying. "If you want change in your life, move twenty-seven things in your house". So she removed twenty-seven objects out of her front entrance. Needless to say, she had huge changes in her career and her friends started coming over to visit her again. There was room to come in her front entrance. There was nothing in her way blocking out her opportunities or her friends. She was happy.

Angels to Call Upon for This Area

Call upon Archangel Chamuel if you are going through a career change. He will help you release the old way of thinking from your life to make way for the new beginnings. He helps us find synchronistic situations that bring in opportunities and the right people. He will help you find the career best suited for your purpose and passion. Call upon him to assist you with your dreams. He will divinely inspire you pointing the way on your higher path. You may not see the entire path but he will light your way.

Archangel Metatron will help you prioritize through sacred geometry. He will help you get organized. He will help you find your calling and your heart's desire. He will help you find your bliss. Finding your bliss will bring in more joy and happiness in your life. Metatron will also help you make choices that support your life's purpose.

Archangel Ariel the elemental angel of air and earth will help you welcome new opportunities. She will help you walk through that door of opportunity. She will let you know when the timing is perfect. With your higher self she will help you move past your comfort zone and let you know it is safe to follow your bliss. She encourages you to keep your focus upon service, and spirit. She will guide you through your career path. She is a master manifesto and she loves to support those who are searching for their life's purpose. Allow Ariel to aid you into bringing your thoughts (air) manifest into form (earth).

Archangel Uriel is the elemental angel of fire. Call upon him and he will inspire you with his fire energy to trust your inner guidance. With his fire of life energy he will aid you to act upon your calling. He will validate when your thoughts and ideas are right. I feel his heat writing this…With his fire energy he will support you to put your thoughts into action. You will be guided on the steps to take. With Uriel you will know what the next step is to take on your path and he will give you the push and passion to take those steps.

Archangel Sandalphon brings you gifts from the Divine. He helps you to receive your goodness. Did you know that it is said that for each of us there are 1,000 lotus leaves on the top of our head. Each lotus leaf represents the gifts and talents that we have. These are gifts no one else on the planet has. These are the gifts and talents we have to share if we choose. Archangel Sandalphon will help you discover these gifts. Heaven is waiting and very patient with us. The Divine wishes that you be filled with joy, filled with laughter, filled with love, and that all your earthly needs will be provided. Call upon Sandalphon and allow yourself to receive.

Meditation for Contacting Your Higher Self

Sit or lie in a comfortable position. Relax completely.......close your eyes......let all tension drain out of your body and mind ....breathe deeply and slowly......relax more and more deeply.

Now imagine yourself standing on green grass. Your feet are growing roots into the earth making you feel grounded. You feel the nourishment and magnetic power of the earth coming up through your body, making you feel totally balanced and grounded. Now this magnificent energy travels throughout your body and up to your heart. Visualize an emerald green light within your heart......glowing radiant and warm. Feel it spreading and growing ......shining out from you farther and farther ......you are a radiating loving energy on everything and everyone around you......

Now imagine you are on a spiral path going upward. You are going on this path to meet your higher self. This is the wise being that dwells within you. As you meet up with your higher self you have a deep sense of knowingness and certainty, of power, love, and wisdom. You both agree to go to the luminous white cloud that is your subconscious. It is the limitless space and time where thought forms are created into matter. While holding the thought of what you desire to manifest, you roll up your eyes as if looking up to the heavens and you silently state you're desire. I don't know how I have the career best suited for my passion and purpose in life.

I only know that I do now and I am fulfilled. You rest in this place for a moment. While still in this space you allow your vision to expand............ your vision becomes greater than you had imagined.

Your higher self-nudges you and tells you to receive. You receive and you feel fulfilled. You clearly state thank you in your mind. You experience a sense of gratitude and fulfillment emanating from your whole being...... your higher self takes you back down the spiral. Back down into your body where you feel an energetic shift in your body on a DNA level. You unwind all of your old limiting thoughts and beliefs. You let them go. And you rewind the new understanding of your manifestation. You say thank you to your higher self. Your higher self tells you can call upon its presence at any time. It is always with you. You see your higher self-fade.......you say thank you again, it is done. It is so. You begin to wiggle your fingers, roll your shoulders and on the count of three you will open your eyes. One you are coming back, two becoming more aware, three opening your eyes. Welcome back to your new path and journey.

Knowledge & Inner Skill

It is time to tap into your knowledge and inner skill area which is located in the front left section of the Bagua map.

This area has earth energy. There are two different kinds of earth energy. There is mother earth and there is mountain earth. This area contains mountain earth energy. The mountain earth energy symbolizes taking the time to climb to the quiet heights within us. This area on the Bagua map brings up the importance of meditation and introspection. This mountain earth energy symbolizes the climb to the quiet heights within us, to that place with our higher self where we can contemplate our experiences and integrate them. This knowledge area affects the mental / inner / spiritual / personal areas of your life. If you have the desire to become smarter or wiser, more spiritual, want to experience personal growth and self-development, this is the area in your life you need to address. This area of your home is the place you need to take a good look at. To become truly knowledgeable is far more complex than simply gathering information. Knowledge is the seed of wisdom and it grows through being nourished by both study and contemplation. Buy yourself some new books, start meditating or start meditating more. Think outside the box. Be courageous and climb the mountain.

This area works hand in hand with your marriage and partnership area of your life. This is because they are situated diagonally across from one another. So if you want to improve your love life or partnerships, start looking at this area of your life so you can get a different perspective on your relationships and your life. Remember everything starts with you.

The knowledge area is also concerned with business data, competitive intelligence, computer networks and good decision making.

If you need to improve any of these areas in your life addressing the knowledge area can help you keep up with the continuous change and flow of information. This information is available to each and every one of us for all of our own individual needs.

The colors for this area are green, blue and black.

To enhance and improve your life you in this area you will need to start with your inner work. A good place to start with is your spiritual growth. A book I recommend for this is *Sacred Contracts* by Caroline Myss. The subtitle is awakening your Divine Potential.

We all have our own sacred contracts or a higher purpose. This book will help you find out what you are here on earth to learn and whom you are meant to be. This book helps you shine light on the purpose and meaning of life and connects you to your shadow side, showing you how not be afraid of yourself. If you embraced your shadow side it will not have control over you. I was in a meditation class years ago where we were going to meet our shadow self. Well, I was scared to death but I did it anyway. When I meet my shadow self it was a handsome being and then I knew it was fear itself that I had been afraid of.

It was April 15th 2002 and I was facing something dark that was growing inside of me for seven years. It was cancer. Once I faced my fear it had no more control over me. I faced it, did what I had to do, and now I am well and healthy.

In Feng Shui we have Yin and Yang or, the dark and the light. Everything in the universe is composed of two opposite yet complementary to themselves. Yin the dark symbolizes the passive side of nature the feminine, while Yang the light represents the active side the masculine. Yin and Yang don't exist independently. Each quality carries the color of its opposite within itself, showing that within all things is the seed for potential change. This concept is an important key to Feng Shui. It is an important key to human nature.

Check out books for your own personal growth. Learn a new language, study the stars, or read about your ancestors. Choose whatever you have always been interested in learning but never gave yourself the time to do. Start exploring now.

In your physical environment if you want to see positive changes improve the interior lighting levels. In design, proper lighting has a huge effect on function and the mood of the area. If the area feels too dark lighten it up. This little change will work magic in your life. You know the old saying of "meeting someone and there were no lights on".

Get rid of things you don't need in this area. In design less is more. Proclaim your independence by clearing and removing your junk. When you clean it increases your freedom and happiness. Especially in this area where you need to make a clear, clean passage for new information to come in and for a new perspective on life and living.

If you want to liven up your life, add a splash of color to add life to this area. The colors of this area are greens, blues, and blacks. The green and blue colors will be adding cheer, life, and growth. The black color will be bringing in introspection

When you want to personalize this area of knowledge and inner skill bring in books, tapes, and other materials being studied.

Hang on the walls posters, paintings, collages, and photos of mountains and quiet places. This will inspire and create an invitation for you to go into that place of peace and harmony in your life.

Place statues or figures of teachers and wise people you would like to bring into your life for inspiration and guidance. An example would be a statue of Quan Yin who represents compassion or a stature of saint Francis of Assisi who guides you to follow your heart. Use a statue of Jesus to open your heart. I carried a statue from Fatima, Portugal of Mother Mary all over Europe to bring home to my mother in 1972. Today my mother has since passed. She was almost 99 years old. But while she was living she felt nurtured by the presence of Mother Mary in her home.

If it feels appropriate put up pictures of teachers or mentors that you admire and aspire to be like. These types of pictures are perfect to put in this area of your home.

Place anything that has a personal association to knowledge and self-cultivation. I have an Asian screen depicting life's beautiful journey in this area of my home. This feeds the Angelic Feng Shui journey that I am on.

Quotes, affirmations, and inspirational sayings pertaining to knowledge and self-cultivation are wonderful to place in this area. Place inspirational sayings from people you admire in this area. This will help you create a new reality for yourself. If it says something wonderful and inspirational place it where you can read it and have it become part of who you are.

Sometimes in life what is unseen is more real than that is seen.

Some affirmations that you can write down and place them in this area for yourself are:

- I trust my learning process

- I am wise and knowledgeable

- I am constantly learning and knowing

- I always know what to say and do.

Write down your own personal affirmations or elaborate on these. If it resonates with you, you know it is right.

The Angels to Call in for This Area

Call upon Archangel Raziel if you want to have spiritual understanding. He will bring you information and symbols, to help you understand spiritual truths. He will help you open up to new ways of looking at life. Work with Archangel Raziel and pay attention the information that comes to you. If it comes to you three times or more it is time to pay attention. Raziel will help you understand the world around you. He will guide you in your dream sleep and will give you knowledge that will help guide you through your awakened state.

Call upon Archangel Zadkiel to help you with clairaudience, the gift of hearing. He will help you hear the loving divine guidance you hear inside your mind. He will help you hear this divine guidance with clarity. It will come in the form of repetitive messages. Ask him for help when you need clarification on information coming in. Call upon him and he will help you keep an open mind and learn new ideas. Zadkiel's aura is a deep indigo blue. The mineral that resonates with him is lapis lazuli. Zadkiel is the ultimate spiritual professor and if you have the gift of teaching he will aid you.

Archangel Metatron is wonderful to call upon to clear and open your chakras (you're energy centers). He uses sacred geometric shapes. He cleanses the toxins from your body and energy centers. When your chakras are clear you'll feel more energized and have increased intuition. When your energy centers are clear it is easier to meditate and think clear for new information to come in. Metatron's aura is beautiful violet and sea-foam-green strips. The crystal that resonates with him is watermelon tourmaline.

There are other angels to call upon for your individual needs. There is an angel for everything. For example, if divine truth is what you are seeking, call upon the angel of truth. If abundance is what you need the angel of abundance, etc.

When I sing I call upon the Seraphim's and Cherubim's. They are singing angels and sing around the throne of God. Their tones and sounds are healing to the human soul. I sing in a choir and when I want to make sure I sing like one voice with the choir I call upon their help. It is very comforting to have back up.

Mountain Meditation

Relax completely in a comfortable position. Close your eyes. Relax your eyes, your teeth, your mouth, and your jaw. Relax your shoulders, your arms, your hands. Relax your chest, your stomach, your buttock. Relax your upper legs, your calf's, and your feet. Take in a deep breath and let it all out and just relax….

Now imagine you are in a beautiful natural green environment. You are standing in a beautiful green meadow. In front of you is a mountain. Take time to imagine all the beautiful details and you see yourself fully enjoying and appreciating your surroundings. You continue to wander and explore and you find yourself with your higher self-going up the mountain path. The path becomes more and more exquisitely beautiful. You come upon a cave. The front entrance is shaped like an old cathedral door. You walk through the front entrance and you realize you are walking into a cave. The walls of the cave are filled with violet white crystals giving off a radiant, warm, glow. You walk further into the cave and you come upon a niche. There is a gift in the niche that has been waiting for you. You pick it up and you are filled with joy and delight and you are grateful for what you have been given. You place it back in the niche knowing that it is always there for you. You walk further on into the cave noticing an opening. There is a luminous white light radiating from the opening. You walk up and up and through to the other side of the cave's opening. You have made it to the top of the mountain. Here you sense that this is where truth and wisdom, peace and love, live. You see at a distance the shining stars sending you a shimmer of golden, white light surrounding you. Everything becomes luminescence white. You are in a cloud of your higher consciousness. You are connected to your divine source. You roll up your eyes and see the top of your head. There are a thousand lotus leaves. These are all your gifts and talents you have. These are all the gifts and talents that only you have and have been given to you in this lifetime. You make a wish and you pick the gift that is outstanding to you amongst the others. I don't know how I am so blessed. I only know that I am now and I am fulfilled. You expand on this vision……….you see all the blessings in your life. You are truly grateful for you are truly blessed. You bring in all the glorious energy and you feel the immense love of the angels surrounding you with their love. You feel blissful like you have never felt before. You stay here for a while……

It is now time for you to leave. You know you can return here any time you wish. As you turn around, you are greeted by Angels who assist you going back through the cave to the main entrance. You thank the angels and you proceed to walk outside of the cave. You find yourself back on the mountain path. This time you are going down, down, down, back to the beautiful green meadow. You feel yourself go back into your body. You wiggle your toes, your fingers. You roll your shoulders……. on the count of three you are coming back…..one, coming back, two, three you open your eyes and you are back.

Health and Family

————◦❧◦————◦❧◦⟐◦❧◦————◦❦◦————

Health and Family are two ingredients for an abundant life. This area can be found at the middle left side of the Bagua map. It is between knowledge and inner skill, and wealth and prosperity. Wood is the element for this area and the colors are green and blue. It addresses the importance of cultivating strong physical health and family connections. Health and family addresses loving family relations and how they affect our health. Family includes ancestors, parents, siblings, blood relatives, and close friends.

Did you know that if you heal yourself you heal everyone in your family on different levels? You can even heal your ancestors energetically. It is believed you can go all the way back to Adam and Eve. This area of our life is very important to our well-being. Loving family relations are a supportive foundation through the periodic shocks and unforeseen storms in our life. These solid foundations of family and health provide for the opportunity for expansion, growth, and happiness in our life. The healthier we are the more options we have to exercise, play, travel, work, and physically enjoy life. Also, the healthier our relationships are with our family and friends, the more we prosper from the emotional support they provide. Disease which means 'not at ease' begins first in your emotional body then manifests in your physical body. Feng Shui saying: "When good physical health and emotional relations are solidly in place, auspicious opportunities are best assured, and inauspicious times are best survived."

To achieve balance of peace and harmony we start with the inner workings of health and family. We use the elements air, water, fire, and earth to heal our mental, emotional, spiritual, and physical bodies. The element of air is to clear the mental self. Look at your core values. Is there a need to change or rearrange these values? Make an inner commitment to live in harmony with your values. Make a list for yourself of your core values. Core values include love, joy, abundance, and spirituality. Create activities in your life to be consistent with your top values so you feel in harmony with them.

Start becoming aware of the quality of air you breathe. You can't have mental clarity without the proper breathing. Become aware of how many times you stop yourself from breathing. Take a walk. Breathe..........

Get rid of internal clutter which is always thinking, rationalizing, worrying, or analyzing, without taking time to be quiet and to listen to your inner voice. You create internal clutter when you have such a busy schedule that you are always overwhelmed. If this resonates with you, start cutting out the clutter in your schedule and allow yourself to breath.

Internal clutter is also created when you're not listening to others. If you are going to speak, think about what you are going to say; speaking your truth from your heart. Take a good look at yourself and see if there is anything you need to change about how you think and talk. Your words are who you are. Do you like what they are saying? Set yourself free and clear your mental self by eliminating internal clutter.

To clear your emotional self, use the element of water. This is an area that a lot of people find hard to clear. When there is an emotional baggage you don't need to go through all of it to release it. You don't go through your physical garbage before you throw it in the trash. The same is true with your emotional baggage. You don't need to go through all of it unless some small part of you wants to hold on to it for whatever reason. Ask help from your guides and angels to assist you in releasing that which no longer serves you. Releasing old hurts and stories allows space for joy and love. Releasing old hurts and stories allows you to start living in the present. I went to a retreat recently and a tool the nun who was leading the retreat gave us for releasing old hurts and stories was very simple. The tool was a thought to keep in your head. This thought was that when you have an issue with someone and have been caring the hurt or anger maybe a year, a month, a day, or an hour in that time you don't know what has transpired between that person and their maker. To keep this thought the next time you see that person you can always have a fresh start with them. You can stay in the present. Become courageous and when you do you will see miracles unfold in your life.

Another technique to help eliminate recurring negative emotions is to write down the sad stories (events) that have occurred in your life. Then, read them aloud to yourself in the mirror or another person.

Keep reading them over and over until you can read the stories without crying. When you first read your stories allow yourself to sob. They will feel real as if they are happening to you at the present moment. After all, they are your stories and what you identified with on who you are. We all identify with our stories. Each time you read your stories, you will cry less. By the time you read your stories the fourth or fifth time you won't cry and you may even start laughing in some parts. They now have become just past stories. They aren't happening to you in the present moment. You won't feel the emotional charges when reading your stories. They are just stories. You are being really brave. When you do this technique you will release the past, stand in the present and allow yourself to feel who you really are – a loving person made perfect in the image of God.

Another technique that is very easy is to use the water element. Take a bath or shower and mentally wash your hurts, disappointments and sadness down the drain. Water has the wonderful properties of detoxifying and clearing out negativity. You can also go to the beach and the salt water will cleanse your emotions and give you a natural high.

To clear your spiritual self, use the element of fire. Activate the spirit of fire that dwells in and around you by focusing on your inner light and physically going out into the sunlight. Breathe in the light of the sun. Remember the rainbow energy of the sun energizes your spiritual essence. Step into a state of trust and faith. Visualize, feel or just know that the light within you is ready to expand and become even more vibrant and glowing. Activate the inner light that is the fire within. You can do this with thought. For this to come about you will need to step out of your comfort zone and challenge yourself. Break a habit today. Say yes to life. And no matter what is happening in your life find a way to create fun and joy! Turn on the music and dance. Do this and you will clear your spiritual self and your spirit will soar. You might even feel your angel wings.

When clearing your physical self, use the earth element. This planet earth has everything you need to maintain and support your physical health. Your physical body is your tool for experiencing the world. It allows you to feel, taste, touch, smell, hear and see everything around you. Your body and the earth are constantly communicating with you. Start listening to the messages of your body. An example of a simple message of the body: if it is telling you that it is full, listen and stop eating. If it is saying I am thirsty, start drinking more water. If you feel sluggish, listen, maybe you need to detoxify your body. If this is the case eat lighter and eat lots of raw organic vegetables and salads. Drink detoxifying herbal teas or green teas. Drink more water and water with a squeeze of lemon. Adding lemon to your water helps balance the acidity and ph. levels in your system. Keeping your body cleansed is crucial to your health. If your body is stagnant and sluggish it is easy to feel emotionally, physically and mentally stagnant. When your body is vibrant, you are vibrant. Listen to the messages of nature and become in tune with your life force. The earth has healing powers. A Bishop friend was consulting with the Pope prior to becoming a bishop. The Pope told the bishop that if he wanted to hear, see, feel, messages from God he needed to go out into nature. Take yourself as much as you can out in nature and connect with the earth. This will awaken the natural forces within you.

Address this area of health and family when you want to improve your health, when you are recovering from surgery, or if you are playing in sports.

This is also the area to address if you would like your friends and your "family of choice" to grow or improve. It is an important area for your relationships with relatives to improve.

In your physical environment if you want to see positive changes in this area bring in nature. Nature is the perfect area to bring into the home to maintain health and balance. A simple remedy is to put a big beautiful healthy plant in the room. This will represent your vibrant health. Also bring in fresh flowers with vibrant colors and smells. Put up a photo of nature or create an arrangement of leaves, pinecones, feathers, and stones in a bowl as a playful display. Bring in the music of nature through sounds such as raindrops, ocean, wind, birds and so on.

For optimum health choose art that you associate with optimum health and place it in this area. I was commissioned to do a water color painting of an angel for a person who was terminally ill with cancer. She came to me a year later and wanted to meet me to tell me she looked at the painting every day and she healed. A copy of that watercolor is on page 146.

Bring in the colors of all the five elements together: green, red, yellow, white, and black. This powerfully invokes harmony and balance. Bring in a beautiful display of different colored candles. Make sure fresh air is flowing in and out of this area and it is totally de-cluttered. Fresh air flowing in and out and keeping the area clear of clutter will maintain a healthy mental state.

The health and family area concerns your nuclear family as well as all your relatives and close friends. Work on this Feng Shui area to resolve interpersonal family conflicts or to promote family harmony. If you would like your relationship with relatives to improve and to feel more love within your family, display endearing pictures of them with smiles on their faces. Go through old albums and frame the happiest, loving pictures. Bring in this energy. If you can't find any pictures like this, then cut happy family pictures out of magazines. This will work, too.

Put up quotes, affirmations, and sayings pertaining to the ideal family. An example of an affirmation is: I enjoy wonderful relationships with my family, or I enjoy harmonious relationships with my friends, or I am blessed with vibrant health and loving relationships.

For harmonious loving relationships with family and friends you can also bring in other items that have a personal association to family, such as mementos, heirlooms, etc.

If you are having emotional issues that are interfering with having healthy relations check your home's plumbing (dripping faucets, clogged drains). Clogged drains symbolize a difficulty releasing old things. The cure is easy. Clear the pipes! Leaking pipes also correspond to kidney issues. Any leak in the house creates a loss of energy and a loss of your wealth. So fix your leaky faucets, problem toilets, and faulty pipes A.S.A.P.

If you are having family and health problems look to see if you need to correct any foundation problems in your home. This includes foundation defects and cracks, earthquake damage, and water infiltration. These problems can cause family and job instability and can bring health problems.

If you are having a problem with your nervous system, the system that correlates to the body's nervous system is your home's electrical system. Fix any faulty wiring, lights, fuse boxes, transformers, computers or phone lines. These fixes can help eliminate physical problems including memory loss, irritation, muscle spasms and even more serious nervous system issues.

Check the roof of your home as it relates to both the head and the back. If you have any leaks or holes it is best to fix immediately. Need I say any more?

Incorporate the energy of wood to bring positive results to your health and family. Wood energy is the energy of expansion and growth. Wood is good to apply when you want to add the energy of expansion, growth, and vitality in your life. It is associated with new beginnings. Wood cures are like adding a touch of spring; the season you feel young, energetic, and motivated. Enhancements that bring in the element of wood in this area are all things that are made from wood, including furniture and decorations. The wood element is found in plants, flowers, floral print upholstery, wall coverings, art depicting landscapes and items in the colors of green and blue.

The Angels to Call in for This Area

When you feel grief you can call upon Archangel Azrial. He will be there for you when you have a loved one that passes over. He is with you in your time of need, helping you to heal your heart. He will give you signs if you ask for them and help you with signs from your loved ones. Azrial's aura is a beautiful shade of vanilla: a very pale yellow tone. He surrounds grieving and dying persons with this loving light to bring them comfort. The crystal creamy yellow calcite is aligned with Azriel's energy. He wants you to let go of your worries and feel loving blessings from heaven.

Archangel Raguel helps you with relationship harmony. He helps resolve arguments and conflicts. He opens up the hearts of everyone involved. If you have his help your prayers for peace will be answered because he has the power to resolve disputes. The meaning of his name is Friend of God. His aura is pale blue and his related crystal is aqua aura or aquamarine.

Archangel Raphael is the Archangel for a healthy lifestyle. The meaning of his name is "He who heals". His specialty is healing physical illnesses and in guiding healers. He helps you to release old patterns that no longer serve you. He will help you to eat a healthful diet, and get exercise and adequate sleep. Ask Raphael to surround anyone needing healing with his emerald green aura. Give your cares and worries to him. If you ask him he will take your burdens and heal your energy. Crystals related to Raphael are emeralds and malachite.

For protection and guarding you and you loved ones and home call upon Archangel Michael. He will surround you and your loved ones, and home with a powerful loving light. With Michael's sword he will defend you cutting away anything negative. You can also ask that he clear your home of any toxic energy. He is God's main protector and after you call upon him you will have a secure feeling. His aura is royal purple and his crystal is sugilite.

For inner peace and harmony call upon the Seraphins. The Seraphins are the angels that sing around the throne of God. Ask them to bring in angelic tones to balance out your chakra centers. They will surround you with their diamond white light. Open up your heart to them and they will fill your heart with love and light. Diamonds are their stone.

For family healing you want to call upon the Cherubim's. They help guard " The tree of life". Like the Seraphins they sing around the throne of God. They are part of the angelic choir. Ask them to intone you in their sweet harmony. The Cherubim are represented to have the likeness of youths.

Meditation to Heal with Tone

Place yourself in a relaxed position, either sitting or lying down. Close your eyes, Relax your feet, your ankles, your calves, your knees, you thighs, and your buttocks area. Relax your body up through your trunk, arms, fingers, neck, and head. Now connect with the magnetic power of the earth. Draw the earth energy up into your feet, up your body, feel it surrounding your heart. The heart energy starts to reach out into the universe, expanding in all directions. Take in a deep breath, breathing in love, and exhale, releasing all negativity.

Now imagine and picture yourself in a cloud of white luminescence white light, the vital energy field of all that is…….…… the place of creation. You are being surrounded with a multicolored light. It is a reflecting iridescent white light with green, blue, and coral colors. These colors swirl around you….. You take yourself through beautiful double doors that are before you. You walk through. There are shimmering lights that dance and sparkle everywhere. As you proceed in this beautiful space you feel the strength of your body, mind, and soul becoming stronger. Right before you reach what looks like a tiered altar, you see beautiful angels. Their wings are glowing, their faces shine, and they are looking at you with love, compassion, and understanding.

You stand there filled with boundless love and you begin to hear music. It is not only outside of you, but resonating on the inside of you. It is as if every cell of your body is filled with this glorious sound. The music is not loud but pulsating and healing. You feel so full of the love of God and this heavenly choir. These angels are the Cherubim and the Seraphim. They are filling you up with heavenly sounds and vibrations. The music is tuning up your DNA for complete wellness, harmony, and peace. It is healing every cell in your body. You stand there for a while and feel the bliss.

Now you feel it is time for you to leave. You slowly turn around and go back through the double doors. As you are leaving you hear the faint sound of the angels. You pass through the white luminescence energy field of creation and you move your consciousness back down a golden beam of light, you come gently and respectfully back into your body. You experience a sense of gratitude and wellbeing emanating from you. You say thank you……and on the count of three you will be back. One, you are coming back, two, you feel your body, three, you open your eyes and you are back.

Wealth and Prosperity

A bundance means different things to different people. For this area of your life wealth and prosperity is located at the rear, top, left section of the bagua.

The wealth corner of your home always depends on the entrance of your home. The wealth corner of individual rooms of the home depends on the entrance into the room. The corner will always be the left corner. The colors of this area are blue, red and purple. This area is associated with the sun which is fire energy. This sun fire energy influences the wind and the wind influences the slow shaping of a rock. The analogy here is that when we take our time shaping our wealth through self-control and patience we are more likely to enjoy each day, while at the same time financially securing our future. My ninety-five year old father lived his life like this. He retired at 55 years old and had seven children. When he died he left my mom who almost reached the age of 99 feeling very secure and my brothers and sisters feeling abundant. In today's society everyone wants instant gratification. They take high risks and like the high winds the results can be unpredictable. Because of this factor the wealth corner holds the potential of bringing fabulous gains or devastating losses.

According to Feng Shui the gradual and steady accumulation of wealth is the best path for securing present and future happiness.

Happiness and abundance comes to us in many forms and means different things to different people. Some people feel abundant because they have close friends and that is what they value most in life. Some people value having good health and having this makes them feel abundant. In Feng Shui when we have the gift of gratitude for the people, places, and things in our lives we most definitely attract more into our lives that bring the experience of abundance and prosperity.

Address this wealth area or enhance your wealth area when you want to bring in more money and material abundance in your life, when you want to raise money for a special cause, or when you want to become more aware and have gratitude for the abundance in your life.

The inner work done in this area is very simple. It is to have gratitude for the all wonderful people and all the wonderful things that are in our life. When we have gratitude we allow the universe to give us more blessings and it opens our hearts for receiving. An exercise for gratitude could be to write down all the reasons why you love your husband or wife or certain friends. Write down all the things in your life that you are grateful for. What you focus on is what you get more of in life. It is the law of attraction. If you don't like certain things in your life think about that another day and just focus on what you like now. Have discipline with this and you will become the master of your own destiny and wealth.

At the time of my dad's passing there was a plum tree centered in his garden patio. When he died the plum tree was loaded with plums. The tree kept giving and giving. We kept giving and giving bags of plums to friends and family. The lemon tree in the front of his home was also loaded with lemons and still is. All my brothers and sisters felt our dad was sending us a message from heaven showing us how blessed and abundant we are.

When my dad passed I would also wake up in the morning and look outside my kitchen window and see all the grapes hanging from the arbor in our side yard. I would see every morning how they were turning a luscious red, purple color. This truly made me feel how rich life is. This is my area of friends and family and when I saw all the grapes it reminded me how blessed I am with wonderful friends and family. These are just some examples which have touched me. I know you have rich stories, too! Take the time to look around you and smell the roses. Allow yourself to feel the richness of life. I remember being in Ireland during the month of June and feeling this richness because everything was so green, luscious and beautiful……….

The gift of the wealth and prosperity corner is the gift of gratitude. When you embrace this gift the universe will be pouring its abundance out to you. Be open to receiving.

A quote from Buddha: "We are shaped by our thoughts; we become what we think. When the mind is pure, joy follows like a shadow that never leaves."

In your physical environment if you want to see positive changes in this area of your life check where the wealth corner in your home or business is and what you have in it. A client's home whom I was visiting told me she had a terrible time with the money flow coming into her household. I immediately saw that her wealth corner was in an outside enclosed patio of the home. She had two huge dogs using the wealth corner of her home for their poop deposits. We changed that right away. She has had no problems with wealth ever since.

People will literally tell me that they throw their money away. I look in their wealth corners and find they have trash cans in them. Isn't it funny how that works?

Remember whatever you put in your wealth corner you will get more of. Remember also that wealth means different things for different people. My first Feng Shui teacher from China had wanted to make money traveling and teaching Feng Shui all over the world. She always felt like she was like a bird so she put a golden bird cage with foreign currency on the bottom of the cage and placed it in her wealth corner. She placed a bird representing herself on the top of the cage symbolizing that she was free to fly. Needless to say, today she flies all over the world, teaches Feng Shui and is richly rewarded.

One of my students had a friend call and told her that she was desperate for money. She had lost her job and was about to sell her jewelry. My student/friend immediately wanted to help and asked her the location of her wealth corner and what was in it. Her friend who lived in Palm Desert, two hours away said it had a lot of stuff in it. Because my student wanted to do what she could for her friend she drove to her friends the next day. When she arrived she immediately went to the wealth corner of her friend's home. It was stacked with old stuff animals, cob webs, and debris. My friend removed all the items out of the corner, sweeping and cleaning the whole space. She told her friend that what she placed in the corner represented wealth to her. Her friend liked fish. So, they placed fish figurines in the corner. The next day after they Feng Shui'd the wealth corner the friend went to the bank to go 'fishing' in her dad's safety deposit box that he had left for her after his death. Inside was an old bank book. Thinking that the book was outdated, but out of curiosity, she handed it to the teller. She discovered there was $42,000 dollars in the account that was now hers. She was ecstatic. After this wonderful surprise she went home. When she checked her mail that day she got a letter from the unemployment office extending her unemployment benefits. A day later she received a check from an old boyfriend who wanted to send her money because he felt guilty. My friend was so excited to share this incredible story with me because it felt so unbelievable and it happened within a couple of days. It was magical. You could say it could be a coincidence but I think different.

I visited a client who wanted to know where the wealth corner was in her home to increase her cash flow. The wealth area was in her kitchen nook and her wealth corner was the furthest left corner of the room. This was great because food and dishes on a dining table represent wealth. We put a large, decorative bowl of fresh fruit in the center of the table. We also placed a large mirror in the room reflecting the table doubling the bowl of fruit and dishes which multiplies wealth. We placed a mirror above her stove making a reflection and doubling all the burners on the stove. This symbolizes doubling your money. We then placed a beautiful healthy green plant in the farthest left corner of the room. Plants are growing energy and it is a lovely way to generate growth in your financial situation. (If your wealth corner doesn't have enough light to support a plant get a real looking artificial plant. This works also.) In the pot of the plant we placed a red envelope with a check she wrote out to herself. I also told her to place nine one dollar bills in the red envelope. To amplify the intention we placed a citrine crystal in the wealth area. Citrine is a money crystal and one of the two minerals on the planet which does not hold and accumulate negative energy. It is one of the stones called the 'merchant's stone' for it not only assists in acquiring wealth but helps to maintain the state of wealth.

After we addressed the wealth area in the home we went outside and in the wealth corner in her back yard. I suggested she buy four small wooden bird houses with red roof tops and place them in the four trees. The bird houses represent all the money coming in. You can also plant a red or purple bouginvia in this corner or any red or purple plant.

She wanted to emphasis money flowing into her life. I explained to do this she would need to address every wealth corner in her home. From the entrance of every room it is always the furthest left corner. I especially wanted her to address the wealth area of her bedroom which is a major money zone. We spend about a third or more of our lives in our bedroom which powerfully influences our monetary life. In my bedroom to address this I have a large Feng Shui beautiful decorative money coin hanging on my wall with a red silk string. In the wealth corner for her we placed a wind chime. This was a great cure for her because it activated this desired area.

A week later I got a call from her ….she explained "Oh my goodness money is coming in from all directions". Money in the mail came from an inheritance that she had forgotten about, extra money from her husband's business, and money from clients she hadn't expected.

More ways to increase wealth and stimulate cash flow is to make sure you are not missing this area of the Bagua.

It is very important that you balance the shape of your house if you are missing the wealth corner. Line up the outer walls of your home and where the imaginary lines of the walls meet complete the corner with a potted plant, tree, fountain, statue etc. I tell people to bury crystals or to place something stationary. If the imaginary lines meet on cement, place a red pot with a red/purple plant or paint a symbol on the cement symbolizing the point of the walls meeting to complete the corner. Use red, purple, and blue colors to complete this area. My sister Maria swears by her red bouginvia in her wealth corner. When it is thriving her business is thriving.

Make sure the front pathway of your home is unblocked. Keeping this path clear allows more energy to enter and circulate in your home and more importantly it allows energy to circulate in the wealth areas of your home. Clear the path for wealth to enter.

Water in Feng Shui signifies your wealth. Flowing water creates your cash flow. Make sure water is always flowing towards your home. Water flowing away from the home symbolizes the loss of money. My parents had neighbors a few years ago who built a fountain in front of their home with the water flowing away from the home towards the street. When I saw this I felt very sad. Within about six months or so they lost their home and had to move.

Since water represents money make sure the plumbing in your home is in good working order. Fix leaky faucets and leaky pipes. Keep drains inside your home like sinks, tubs, and showers plugged or covered when not in use. You heard the old saying "money down the drain". I place decorative sea shells over my drains. And always keep the toilet seat covers down. That is a huge opening for energy to go down the drain. Do this and start visualizing your wealth increasing.

A few other tips are to make sure your mailbox is visible for income and wealth to come in. An invisible mailbox is an energy barrier to receiving income and wealth and a way of sabotaging yourself. Use the colors in this area that represent fire and the energy. The color purple represents wealth, royalty, great energy and power. The color red brings in the energy of power, protection, energy, and activity. The color blue will help you feel lucky. You will feel that the sky is limitless, with life, hope, knowledge, and opportunities. Animal prints represent the fire energy and will work well in this area.

The Angels to Call Upon for This Area

Call upon angels to help you with your financial flow. The angel Abundantia carries a cornucopia of golden coins, which trail behind her wherever she goes. She is the beautiful Roman goddess of prosperity, success, and abundance. Years ago I was told about her and asked her for a sign. I love presents and the next day when I went to work I received unexpected gifts from fellow designers and a business opportunity with extra money. I knew and felt she was around giving me signs and support. So if you ask her for help expect unforeseen windfalls and gifts. One sign that she is with you is that you will find lots of spare change in unlikely locations. Abundantia brings more than just pocket money to those that call upon her; she also brings and bestows all kinds of prosperity. She will bring you new ideas, an increased amount of time, and other forms of support.

The next angel of abundance you can call upon is Archangel Sandalphon. He brings you gifts from God and lets you know your prayers have been answered. He aids you to be rich in consciousness and manifestation in knowing that the future is taken care of in a positive way. He will guide you in appreciating all the miracles and successes in your life. He assists you in knowing that your creator wants you to have all your earthly needs be provided for. Call upon him in allowing yourself to receive. His aura and crystal are turquoise.

Another angel of abundance is the Archangel Ariel. She is known as the Archangel of prosperity and she carries a cornucopia of treasure. She asks you to open your heart to receive. When you call upon her she will shower your life with opportunities and insight. She will guide you to be courageous. A lot of us fear success and how powerful we truly are. Ariel will work her divine magic and miracles will occur. Ariel's aura is pale pink. The crystal that resonates to her energy is rose quartz crystal. Let her love surround you and ask her for whatever you need and she will help you change your dreams into reality.

Meditation for Prosperity

Place yourself in a relaxed position, either sitting or lying down. Close your eyes. Relax your feet, your ankles, your calves, your knees, you thighs, and your buttocks area. Relax your body up through your trunk, arms, fingers, neck, and head. Now connect with the magnetic power of the earth. Draw the earth's energy up into your feet, your body; feel surrounding your heart. Reach out into the universe; expand in all directions. Take in a deep breath, breathing in love, and exhale, releasing all negativity. Your higher self joins you and you are both in a Lovely, natural environment...... a green open meadow with a lovely brook........ Take time to see all the beautiful details, and see yourself fully enjoying and appreciating your surroundings....... Continue to wander and explore......finding it becomes more and more exquisitely beautiful...... take a little more time to appreciate it. Now visualize yourself returning home......it is an enchanted and rich environment that you have created and that suits you. Imagine having loving family, friends, and community around you. Visualize yourself doing work that you love and that richly rewards you. You are appreciated by the people around you and you know that this is an abundant universe with plenty for all of us. You know that abundance is your true state of being and that you are now ready to accept it fully and joyously. You feel in every DNA cell in your body that financial success is coming to you easily and effortlessly and that you are now enjoying financial prosperity. Because you are rich in consciousness and manifestation you know you can return to this state of bliss and state of knowing at any time....... When it is time you slowly and gently come back into your body. You experience a sense of gratitude and wellbeing. You say thank you...... on the count of three you will be back. One, you are coming back, two, you wiggle your toes, your ankles, your fingers, your shoulders, three, you open your eyes and you are back.

Fame and Reputation

When you want to enhance your reputation this is the area to address. The fame and reputation area is located in the middle back part of the Bagua between wealth and prosperity, partnership and marriage.

This area affects your fame and acclaim, such as a Hollywood type of fame and also a more practical side, your personal reputation. This area represents how you are presenting yourself to your family, friends, peers and community. All of us have a reputation. If we have a good reputation it brings many benefits into our lives but if it is a poor reputation it creates huge stumbling blocks on our life's path. When we have a good reputation, warm relationships are all around us giving us the best opportunities for a secure and happy future? We are trusted and we keep our word. Our life is full of good will and we create a good reputation that is assured. We open up our world to the best opportunities and blessed connections.

But if we pay no attention to creating a positive reputation with friends and community, our future is jeopardized.

The element associated with this area is fire "clinging fire". One of the attributes of fire is that it clings to whatever it is burning. So like fire our reputation whether good or bad is impossible to simply shake off. It clings tight, putting us in the hearts of others either warming or burning them. It is our choice to choose what we want people to think about us. This is not to discourage you but sometimes we are unaware that we sabotage our reputation. That is where Feng Shui comes in to aid you and give you the tools.

The fame area influences how you envision your life. Remember the story of Scrooge. That is an extreme example but look how he turned his reputation around. It is never too late to focus on what you want or how you want to re-create yourself. To re-create who or what you want to be known for. The fun thing about Feng Shui is that nothing is sealed in cement. We can get another perspective on things, people around us and most importantly ourselves. How magical is that. Heaven just wants us to be happy. What a concept.

You can enhance or change your fame or reputation area. This area will help you to become well known for an achievement, or to be recognized in different areas of your life by your family or community.

The color associated with this area is red. Red is the most active of all the colors. The attributes that are associated with red are power, protection, energy, and activity. It is the color of your blood, your life force. Let this wonderful color start working for you and become its ally. Put on your red and let's begin with your inner work for this area of your life.

When we are children we know exactly who we want to be, what we like, and how we want to show up. What I'd like you to do is to go back to your childhood and remember who you wanted to be like, how you liked to play, and how you wanted others to see you. When I was young I loved watching Shirley Temple movies. I wanted to be like her. She was always singing and dancing. She was always concerned and nice to people. Today I sing in a choir, dance with my husband, and it always feels good to be nice. I also watched Loretta Young on TV and was so mesmerized with her on how she presented herself. She was always elegantly dressed when she appeared on TV. She exuded grace, charm, and self-confidence in speaking with everyone. When I film my Feng Shui classes or go on TV interviews I aspire to be like her.

When I was about six I remember having tea parties with my dolls. I would pretend to teach school in a little tent in our back yard. When I was about eight I created an angel play with myself dressed up as an angel with angel wings. The next door neighbors had a back yard stage and I held the play there. The admission price to see the play was a penny or a button.

Well today as an adult I teach Feng Shui classes in my home. I offer tea and munchies and have a tea party like I did with my dolls. I don't dress up as an angel and put on a play but I do bring in and work with angels while I am teaching class.

My life was influenced by my parents. My mother was loving, warm, and kind. My father's wise advice was that if I didn't have anything nice to say, say nothing at all. Those were tall orders. He taught me how to choose friends. He advised me that if someone is talking badly about another person soon they would be speaking poorly of me. These were not friends I wanted. He taught me to choose my friends wisely because they were a statement about whom I was and they would have an influence on which I was to become. I always tell my students you can choose to be around saints or sinners it is your choice.

The powerful work you can do in this area of your life is to watch what you say. Your word is who you are. What are you saying about yourself? If it isn't nice stop yourself from saying it. Are you true to your word? How do you show up? Make sure you follow through with what you say you will do. Recently I promised three teenage girls I would gift them with something I had made. They saw me wearing feather earrings and they loved how they looked. They even gave me the colors they would like. The following week when I saw them again and brought the gifts they were all surprised and each one said they didn't think I would really do it. I was surprised. I gave them my word. I then realized that it was the greater gift of trust that I had given them and the physical gift was just the vehicle.

In your physical environment if you want to see positive changes in your fame treat this area of your home with photos that express who you are. Put up pictures and paintings of inspiration that bring in the qualities that you want to be known for. Bring in the fire element by bringing in some items in the color red. Place things that have personal associations or pertain to fame and reputation such as acknowledgements, awards, trophies, prizes, affirmations, and sayings in this area.

I remember when I first started practicing Feng Shui. I worked part time for a fashion jewelry company. I had just started with the company and within six months they were going to have their annual convention. They were going to give performance awards, trophies and prizes to their employees. So I cut out the pictures of the awards, prizes, and trophies that I desired and placed them in the center of the back wall of my home (my fame and reputation area). I went to the convention. When they first called out my name for the top trophy for my division I was so shocked I fell off my chair, got a huge bruise, and hoppled to the stage to receive my award. I received every prize, award, and trophy that I put up in my fame and reputation area. I even was awarded a real diamond, ruby, and gold ring. I was shocked…..

Now that doesn't always guarantee that what you put in that area will manifest or will come to you there are other influences that affect fame or recognition. One influence is intent. When you intend to achieve and work towards that goal, and you put the effort out the return will usually be in the form of fame or recognition. Sometimes the returns are better than you imagined.

In one of my classes a student wanted to win an award and grand prize money for her garden. I shared my story with her on what I had done. So she cut out a picture of the award and grand prize money that she wanted to win and placed it in her fame and reputation area as if she had already won it. It was so exciting to get the news from her when I came home from a trip. She had won the award, the grand prize money of ten thousand dollars. The picture of her garden was illustrated in the home and gardens section of our local newspaper.

This last story is about how you should be proud of who you are. We are all special human beings who have been blessed with many gifts and talents. It is good to shine and just allow ourselves to be. That is one of the reasons why we came in human form. We came to share our talents and to be of service to one another through love.

This story is about my first Feng Shui teacher, Lillian Gardiner and her friend. The friend called Lillian panicked and said, "Everyone thinks I am a movie star but I haven't had an acting job in years and I am about to lose my home". She asked Lillian to come to her home and Feng Shui it. Lillian went that week knowing the desperate situation of her friend. Lillian straight away went to her friend's fame and reputation area which was her home office. Lillian asked her where the pictures of her were of her being in the movies. She said, "I didn't put them out because what would people think?" Lillian responded, "They will think you are a movie star." They immediately placed well known pictures of her friend in various movies out on her desk. They brought in the star template that she was given after being inducted onto the Hollywood Walk of Fame. They placed it in the center of the back of the room. When they did this the sun shined through immediately. Everyone got the chills. Within two weeks the friend called Lillian and said, "Oh my goodness you saved my home! I am in Ireland and I am in a movie. I have the money to pay my mortgage."

So you see there is nothing you need to change about who you are. It is just the stories and worrying about what other people think. Strive for being the best, most authentic person you can be. Strive to be a kind, loving human and look for the good in your fellow man and it will reflect back to you. Strive to do this and with the grace of God we can make this a better, more loving world to live in.

In conclusion treat this area of your home with inspirational photos, pictures, or paintings of yourself on what you want to be known for. Paint the back wall of this area red or place red color accessories here. Animal prints also work in this area representing fire energy. Place things that have personal association to fame and reputation such as acknowledgements, awards, trophies, prizes, affirmations, and sayings pertaining to fame. Do this and see magic happen in your life.

Angels to Call Upon for This Area

Archangel Haniel will help develop your hidden talents and help you live to your fullest potential. She will give you the passion to guide and lead you to follow your true heart's desire. One of the minerals that are associated with her is the garnet. Garnet is also the stone that is related to the area of fame. With its color as bold as blood it assists you in what you are here to accomplish and what you want to be known for. It clears the path for your creativity and gives you back your passion. When you, Archangel Haniel, and the mineral garnet couple together you will be able to facilitate your shift of awareness to "all that is". This will take you to heights of accomplishments and fulfillment that were once merely your dreams that now you can manifest in your life. How wonderful is that!

The next angel is Angel Oriel. He is the guardian angel of destiny. He will come to help you find your true destiny in life. Destiny can call you at any age. If you feel like your life is changing and you need a career change call on Angel Oriel. It is up to you to make the choice to follow your destiny or not. If you have the courage to embrace your destiny he will aid you with to follow your life's purpose. Ask for a sign that you are on the right path. It has to feel right in your heart. The element associated with Oriel is gold. He is a golden guardian angel. His golden energy of love will aid in logical thought processes, help you review situations, and give you the ability to make informed decisions and to take the appropriate action.

Mother Mary is the Queen of angels. She is angel of wisdom, compassion, love, and faith. She brings in the ancient wisdom. She will aid you in your quest to achieve your true potential and what you want to be known for. There is nothing you cannot accomplish with the power of love and light that she brings. She will help you experience the higher vibrations of love energy, allowing you to transform and re-program the divine blueprint of your life. Her aura is filled with opalescent colors that are predominately blue. Her element is pearl. She comes to help you with new faith, fills you with heavenly love and to rise above your sorrows and achieve your expectations and more.

Meditation…for…Wisdom

Put yourself in a relaxed position, either sitting or lying down. Close your eyes. Relax your feet, your ankles, your calves, your knees, you thighs, and your buttocks area. Relax your body up through your trunk, arms, fingers, neck, and head. Now connect with the magnetic power of the earth. Draw the earth's energy up into your feet, up your body, feel it surrounding your heart. Reach out into the universe, expanding in all directions. Take in a deep breath, breathing in love, and exhale, releasing all negativity. Now imagine yourself creating a pure energy channel that can reconnect you to the earth and to the stars. You open the meridian from your crown chakra right down to your base chakra. You invoke Mother Mary to bring her sacred energies in gold and silver rays of infinite love and compassion. Mother Mary, Mother Mary, Mother Mary, love and light, love and light love and light. She connects your crown to the stars with celestial star fire and the base of your spine to earth with earth fire. As you breathe in these energies, they meet and integrate in your heart. Your heart expands and grows and you feel deeply loved. You absorb the life –transforming rays into your very cells as they begin to heal you. You re-generate your self-belief and zest for life and you determine new aspirations for your future and what you want to be known for. You see or feel these new aspirations very clearly. They were there at your birth. These new aspirations aid you in your quest to achieve your true potential. There is nothing you cannot accomplish with the power of love and light. You continue to experience the gold and silver rays of infinite love and compassion. It is allowing you to transform and re-program the divine blueprint of your life. You stay here for a while with Mother Mary and her sacred energies. You sit here and bask in her radiant energy.

Soon it is time to say goodbye. Know that you can call upon her at any time. As you bring yourself back into your body you begin to feel its sensations again. At the count of three you will be back, one, coming back, two, wiggling your fingers, and your toes, three, opening your eyes and you are back.

Marriage and Partnership

---◆❸⟩··---◆··⟩◆(◉)◆⟨··◆---◆❸◆---

W̲ant to bring more love into your relationships? The love, marriage, and partnership area is the right rear section of the Bagua map or the right rear area of the structure you are working with.

The energy here is of "receptive earth" or "mother earth". The yin (feminine energy) or yielding which is associated with the qualities we find in true love. These qualities are unconditional support, adaptability and devotion. The mother earth's energy stabilizes, balances, and grounds us. Earth helps us become centered and connected to bedrock. It is important to use this earth energy to stay centered and grounded as this affects the quality and status of your marriage and relationships.

We all know how marriage and relationships can become challenging at times. If your marriage or relationships need transformation and growth treat this area to make the necessary changes. If you are looking for that someone special this area affects your ability to find a partner.

For business concerns this is also called the partnership area. It includes your internal business partners such as two people owning a business and your external associates, the individuals who are the key people you engage with to conduct your business.

The colors connected with this area are pink, red, and white.

The color pink represents the heart, love, and marriage. Add the color pink and frame a picture of you and another in a pink heart.

The color red gives the area power, protection, energy, and activity. To bring in the color red, place two red roses in a vase in this area. This energizes and activates romance between two people.

The color white conveys purity of heart and spirit. White also produces righteousness, which connects you to your spirit and God. Plant two white jasmines in the marriage corner of your backyard and this will bring in purity of heart and spirit. This will also add a beautiful scent to this love corner.

In this area of romance and partnerships always place items in pairs. An example would be to place a statue of a woman and man together. I had a client who wanted to get married but when I visited her home there was nothing representing couples. She had single women depicted throughout her home. She didn't realize she was sabotaging her desires.

Enhance your marriage and partnership areas when you would like to attract a love relationship, improve your current love relationship, improve your business partnership relationships, or when you want to improve the relationship with yourself.

The work in this area starts with you. To attract the right partner in your marriage or your business partnership relationships is to be your authentic self. The first step is to call in your higher self and work with your breath. While focusing on your breath call upon your spirit which is your most authentic self and ask yourself ....how is my spirit today? You may feel silly doing this but it works. Take time to listen. See how you feel and see what your needs are. When you are ready give it to yourself.

Give yourself a fifteen minute walk, go dancing, sing along with the music, or take a luscious hot bath. Feed your spirit. This will lift your inner self and bring in joy! If your ego stops you for whatever reason, get your ego out of the way and allow yourself willingly to receive from the one person you know intimately.....which is you.

The ego is finite and our spirit has endless possibilities. The spirit sets us free. A way of getting into the spirit is through your breath so start focusing on your breathing. Two years ago I went on a ten day retreat. The retreat was how to breathe and feel the connection with spirit through breathing. You don't have to go to a ten day retreat to experience this but what you can do is give yourself time in the morning to focus on your breathing and call spirit in. Pop out of ego with breath......... clear your throat with three coughs and breathe.......lead by your spirit and heart.

For those that have a marriage partner or would like to get married this area will create union. Marriage from man's beginning has been a sacred union. God made marriage a sacrament. A sacrament, as we know, is an outward sign that gives us an inner grace. It is God's design that man and woman complete each other, draw strength from each other, so we can contribute to one another's spiritual growth.

Our main purpose of marriage besides raising children is to help each other to get to heaven. The union between two people is the highest form of love to God.

But no matter how well matched there are difficulties that arise causing a lack of clear communication. Ask yourself, "How I am communicating with my partner?" Am I telling him or her my feelings or needs? Am I telling them what would make me happy? Am I asking what their feeling and needs are? Am I asking what would make them happy? Communicate today with your partner and when you communicate also make sure you have a clear heart. Limit communication when you have a negative emotional heart. Emotions change and you can never take back what you have said. Give yourself space and be clear. Speak your truth from your heart.

When I am upset with my husband I always give myself space instead of immediately responding to him. This way I give myself time to get the emotions out of the way. I go to another room sometimes say a little prayer which really changes the energy to a higher vibration (even if I wanted to stay mad it is hard to) or I will wait till the next day if needed. This allows me time to act instead of react and to be able to communicate with a clear heart.

When you are emotional and upset you tend to blame, shame and criticize the other person. They then will return the favor of blame, shaming, and criticizing. This gets neither of you anywhere but hurt.

Take responsibility for yourself and don't blame, shame and criticize the other person but say instead "I can't handle this "or "I feel hurt." You are not putting it on the other. You are taking responsibility for your own feelings. In the end it is not about who is right or wrong but about how we treat each other.

Sometimes our vibration and frequency isn't matching. Nobody is wrong. You are just listening to another tune. You are on different wave lengths you might be listening to jazz music while they are listening to classical. Don't take things personal but try with your whole heart to look at things objectively. This will help stop the misery.

Whenever you feel stuck make sure that the lines of communication are open with your partner. Call in your higher self to assist you with this. Having a heart to heart talk is the quickest way to bring back the romantic feelings that bought you together. The truth will set you free and bring you the love and joy you deserve.

With business partnerships also make sure the line of communications are open. Have a heart to heart talk with your business partners and speak your truth. The truth in this case will also set you free.

In your physical environment if you want to see positive changes in this area of your life start bringing in the right colors.

Start with your master bedroom. This area should have very yin energy (feminine energy). I once taught an entire class of women that were having problems with their marriages. We immediately went to their master bedrooms and I gave them treatments that would bring back the love and romance with their husbands. Your master bedroom should be a sensual place where your entire senses are celebrated. Your bed should be the center piece and be graced with bedding that consists of sensuous fabrics fit for a queen or king. The surrounding pictures in the room should be filled with romantic life. Make the art absolutely wonderful from the view from your bed. Couples that share the same view from the bed share the same view in life. Make sure that the art above the bed is very pleasing. Because if you think about it that is the last thing you see before you go to sleep. Make it something you would like to dream about. The master bedroom is the place for just you and your lover.

This is not the place for pictures of children and parents. If you have them in this area please move them. Your romantic life will improve if you do so. Also add romantic music and scented candles. Make it cozy. This is your sanctuary to feel completely secure and sheltered from the world. Make sure there are nightstands on both side of the bed. They don't have to match but be about the same size. On one side of the bed you can have a rectangular shape night stand (masculine energy) and on the other side of the bed a circular shape night stand (feminine energy).

If you are a person that visually needs equal balance pick both nightstands to be the same shape. The shape does not matter as much as making sure you have two night stands. The two night stands symbolically represents that you are inviting each other into your life. If you have to have a TV in the master bedroom make sure it is not in a commanding position. That it is not pulling your energy to always be watching TV. The TV should be in a position that allows you to make that choice of watching it or not. This way it will not be distracting you from what is more important to your wellbeing like your relationship to yourself and your lover.

Make sure you do not have exercise equipment or a desk that you work at in your bedroom. This is your area for rest and rejuvenation.

Lastly, make sure you don't have too many mirrors in the room. This will keep you awake when you need to sleep. I once had a client move into a new home and complained that ever since she moved into her new home she wasn't able to sleep. I went into her bedroom and there was a huge mirrored double door closet that she was facing every night when she went to bed. This was keeping her awake. It was too much energy. She loved the doors so we decided that she would keep them, but we installed a noninvasive drapery rod across the length of the mirrored closet doors for when she needed to sleep. The drapery elegantly flanked both sides of the closet during the day and during the night she draped the mirrors with the beautiful fabric. Well she immediately started sleeping again and started loving her new home.

See how sensual you can make your master bedroom and celebrate all your senses. Tonight make a cup of hot chocolate or drink something delicious in bed. How sweet is that...? Pleasant dreams.........

I am going to share a personal story about the treatments and enhancements I used to create the marriage that I have today. I had been married before and I remember the priest asking me what took me so long to get divorced. To me it was devastating to go through the process. I remember going under my bed covers a lot wishing I would not wake up to this new reality of being divorced. I would take long walks on the beach and concentrate on bringing in joy to replace the pain. I also did this with concentrating on my breathing. I would breath in the fresh air six counts, hold six counts, and breath out six counts……while doing this I would repeat a mantra in my head…I choose joy. I wanted to take my spirit out of my misery.

It had been two years since my divorce and I knew I wanted to get married again. I wanted to use Feng Shui to make the right choice of partners this time. At first I put the picture of Romeo and Juliet in the far right corner of my bedroom, but then realized even though there was a tremendous amount of love in their relationship they had a tragic ending and that was not what I wanted to manifest.

In this corner you always do things in twos so I replaced the picture with a picture of two love doves and two red roses. I then wrote out and placed in a red envelope my new love story. In re-scripting my life and writing out my new love story I was thanking God for bringing the most wonderful man in my life that totally loved and adored me. It is key here to be in the 'already have' thinking mode than to be in the wanting. If you are in the wanting you will always be an arm's length from the having. So fake it till you make it. I wrote down that I specifically wanted a bald-headed warrior from South Africa, a man's man, someone I could trust and respect. I thanked God for bringing me an intelligent man that knew how to make money and that loved to travel. Then I thanked God again for him and having him in my life for my highest good. When I was finished I placed my story in the marriage and partnership corner in a red envelope with a pink rose quartz on top of the red envelope. I wanted my intention to be amplified with the crystal energy of love. I then decided to let go of the intention, send it off for its manifestation, and forget about it. The key here is to let go of your desire so you don't interfere with its manifestation.

Within the next couple of weeks I started taking dancing lessons and working as a designer in an Interior Design showroom. To my amazement I also started dating. I was happy and my spirit was soaring. It had been two weeks to the day that I scripted out my new love story and that Friday I met my husband. It was a Friday night and a friend from dance class wanted me to meet her at a local restaurant. When I got off work we went directly to the restaurant. Before I could get in the door she introduced me to a ball-headed man that looked to me like the man's man that I had imagined. When we were talking it was as if we were in pink bubble and it felt like there was nobody else around but the two of us. He told me that he was involved in a worldwide men's support group known as the Mankind Project and that they called themselves the New Warriors. He was not from South Africa but this bald-headed, spiritual warrior felt right for me. We spent six hours together; it seemed like fifteen minutes.

Five weeks after meeting him and dating I found out that I had breast cancer that had been growing for seven years. I gave him the choice of not continuing with our relationship because we hadn't known each other that long and I didn't know what was going to happen. I had to have an operation, chemo therapy and radiation. He decided to stay in the relationship and never left my side. I felt that was a sure sign he was heaven sent. We were married two years later.

If you are looking for someone to love or want to recreate and make your love life stronger and more loving you can. You can start by re-scripting your life. Be specific and be careful what you script. One of my students scripted that she wanted to meet the love of her life but that she was not ready for him. She wanted only to meet him. Well she met him, broke up and had to wait a year until they got back together again. She went through a year struggling through what she had manifested but joyfully they got back together again and are now happily married.

When I say be specific and clear about what you are manifesting sometimes we are not complete with our true desires. My first teacher scripted that she wanted to marry someone spiritual. She did get someone spiritual and married him. But that is all she got in her marriage; someone spiritual and the marriage did not last long.

Remember it is best to want the whole package. Choose someone compatible with you mentally, emotionally, spiritually, and physically. This person will not only be your partner in love but your partner financially.

Choose someone with a garden full of flowers and not weeds. Start being what you want to attract. Also let go of all of the old limiting ideas you hold about yourself or your inability to create and manifest. Bring in a new understanding of your manifestation. If you want to improve your relationships imagine a perfect future and see yourself in that future. Let that vision of your realized future guide you and live your tomorrow's dreams today. Create yourself a vision and bring in your future to the present. Move and be with this new understanding of reality. Use the spoken word to live the future in the present. Make the present truly a present. In the back of the book there is a Feng Shui Vision Board process that will assist you to accomplish this.

Another personal story I would like to share happened within the last couple of weeks. Before I wrote this chapter on the marriage and partnership area I took a fresh look at the Bagua area of my own home. The marriage map area was outside the structure of my home.

The back area of my home is in a T shape. I lined up the two outside walls of my home. The corner connecting the two imaginary lines completing this corner is on a walking path. Because of this putting a pot or a plant to connect the corners of the Bagua was not an option.

As a solution I laminated two pink hearts on the cement connecting the imaginary lines drawn from the outer walls of my home for this area. Doing this I joined the two lines and completed this missing area of my Bagua.

I also needed to do a lot of yard work. This time of the year brought a lot of spiders in our yard. I had the gardener take out all the spider webs, dead leaves, and trim bushes, etc. My husband on the weekend hosed down the area and after that I spent four hours fine tuning everything.

I took out all the left over dead debris and two plants that I never liked. Whenever I touched the leaves of the plants they would give me a little scratch. Taking out the plants I realized that they symbolized in our marriage relationship the inescapable faults and personality defects grating upon each other. They were deeply rooted so I took the shears and cut away all the little roots that were binding the plants and keeping them so solidly rooted. It took me a long time but as I was cutting away I was picturing all the little hurts going away not only in our relationship but in all our relationships.

I replaced the unwanted plants with soft loving plants. I also put in loving plants with red and pink flowers.

I went to the nursery and purchased two white jasmine trees that were in one pot and planted them in the corner. Jasmine has beautiful white flowers with a sweet fragrance. I imagined both of us bringing in more sweetness and kindness in our relationship.

Because I trimmed the branches of my neighbor's trees that were hanging over our wall and removed more spider webs along with the branches I could see the two white love birds I had placed on the corner of the top of the wall. Seeing this gave me a joyful feeling. Immediately when I made these changes in my marriage corner in my back yard I felt an energy shift in my relationship. It is softer, kinder and sweeter and I love it.

So if there is anything you want to bring back into your relationship like romance, fun, and excitement this is the area to address. If you do ....you too will love it.

Enhance your marriage and partnership areas when you would like to attract a love relationship, improve the love relationship you have now, improve your business partnership relationships, or improve the relationship you have with yourself so that they are healthy and joyful.

If you want to bring in changes in your marriage put pictures up of both of you in a romantic setting, the both of you traveling, or the both of you just having fun. If it is something new you want to bring into your relationship or to create a new relationship get a picture with two people representing you and another in a setting you love and let your imagination soar.........

Angels to Call Upon for This Area

Call upon Archangel Haniel and she will send you a message of love and light. She will bring you infinite love that will heal you if you call upon her. She will teach you the power of love in all its many aspects. She will teach you true unselfish love and compassion. She offers you the light in her pink mirror to see yourself more clearly. If you look in the mirror using your heart as well as your eyes you will be able to see your true self: the loving being that you truly are. If you can love yourself unconditionally you will be able to love others with faults and all. If you let go of judgment you will be able to see the beauty in all things and you will have found true compassion. When you are extra sensitive to emotions and energies she will help you honor yourself and your feelings. Archangel Haniel's aura is pale pink and her related crystals are garnet and rose quartz.

The next angel is Shekinah. Call upon her and she will guide your earthly love. She will help you let go of low self-esteem or feelings that you do not deserve to be loved or happy. Her radiance will help to heal all wounds caused by love, allowing you to transcend these past hurts so you may find your true love. Invoke angel Shekinah to bless your choice of life partner. When your foundations in this life are happy and secure you can create heaven on earth. Shekinah's aura is white- golden radiance. Her related element is white-gold.

The next angel is archangel Chamuel. He will help you with your soul mate relationship. When you call upon him he will help you bring romance into your life. He will do this by guiding your thoughts and actions. He will help to create wonderful love relationships. He will remind you that only love is real. He will show you how to love. He's very kind, loving, and sweet and you will feel the love when you work with him. Chamuel's aura is pale green and his related crystal is a green fluorite crystal.

Meditation for Love

Put you in a relaxed position, either sitting or lying down. Close your eyes. Relax your feet, your ankles, your calves, your knees, you thighs, and your buttocks area. Relax your body up through your trunk, arms, fingers, neck, and head.

Now connect with the magnetic power of the earth. Draw the earth energy up into your feet, up your body, feel it surrounding your heart. Your heart is reaching out into the universe, expanding in all directions. Take in a deep breath, breathing in love, and exhale, releasing all negativity.

Now go to your sanctuary inside your heart. It could be a room….. A meadow…… a place on the beach……… Imagine rays of emerald and magenta coming into this place in your heart. These emerald/magenta rays begin the process of healing and opening your heart fully, you begin to recognize the beauty in all creation, and your heart starts to flower with true unselfish love and compassion. The contemplation of beauty moves you deeply---this is the sublime breath of the angels communing directly with your heart.

You are offered a pink mirror in order for you to see yourself more clearly. You see your reflection and you see your true self……. a beautiful being that is a reflection of all life created.

You surrender to love and beauty, and allow your heart to be filled with warm, golden rays. This overflows into your surroundings and allows those around you also to be healed and fulfilled, for love transcends and heals all situations. Love sets you free…. You bring in the light to prevail and the love to flower in and around your life.

You stay here until you feel it is time to leave. You know you can come back to this place in your heart at any time. You bring yourself back into your body and you begin to feel its sensations again. At the count of three you will be back, one, coming back, two, wiggling your fingers, and your toes, three, opening your eyes and you are back.

Children and Creativity

Your higher self is calling you to get in touch with your creativity. The Children and Creativity is located on the center right side of the bagua between marriage and partnership and helpful people and travel.

This area is connected to the well-being and progress of your children and your inner child. This area also impacts your creativity. This is the area that awakens the magical inner child in all of us. The magical child has a great imagination and is a dreamer.

This area also affects the quality and clarity of your communication; whether it is artistic or otherwise. In business this area connects to employee's creativity at work.

The element associated with this area is metal and the colors are white and pastels. The white color represents metal and metal represents your mental body.

Your mental body is controlled by the brain's two hemispheres. The right side of the brain is the artistic and the left side of the brain is the logical. The right side of your brain connects you to your creative side and to the Divine. It is a conduit for higher creative insights. It perceives life in all its wholeness and sees life how it truly is. It is timeless and when you work with your right brain you become ageless. A good book I would recommend is *drawing on the Right Side of the Brain* by Betty Edwards.

The colors for this area are pastel colors: pink, blue, green, and yellow. These colors represent and bring in the elements of love, spirit, new growth and joy.

The colors help you bring in the qualities of this area which are generosity, encouragement and pleasure. When we encourage others and children to fully express themselves, we bring pleasure and success to ourselves.

When I teach my classes and I have my students do creative projects like make vision maps or spirit sticks it is a magical experience for me. I experience a transformation in them that is beyond words and I am transformed. This magical feeling also happens when we teach children. It brings a joy and sense of great satisfaction to see children blossom and the same holds true of our own creativity.

Expressing yourself creatively is one of the most powerful ways to enhance your life and bring in vitality of your home. It activates joy, enthusiasm, and participation in life.

When you reawaken your own creativity you reawaken your spirit. Enhance your creativity areas when you feel creatively blocked, when you are working on a creative project, or when you want to improve the well-being and progress of your children or to explore your own inner child.

Learn how to tap into your right brain and discover what makes your spirit soar; whether it be drawing or painting, singing or dancing, re-decorating your home or planting herbs in your garden.

Do you like to write, sew, cook, or bake? Bake a delicious cake and fill up your home with wonderful smells and something that you created to share with friends and family. Do you want to learn a new sport or learn how to play a musical instrument?

The hardest and biggest difficulty you will experience in this is finding time for your creative endeavors. The funny thing is, if you allow yourself to do this you will be more productive at work and have more energy all around.

Another challenge is to learn how to tap into the right brain and get out of your left brain. Your left brain is dominant and will try to talk you out of being creative and getting into spirit. The ego is very good at presenting reasons like you need to wash the car, you need to call your mom, or you need to work more. You don't have time to enjoy yourself. You don't have time for fun. The left brain, controlled by the ego is finite and was created to be our faithful servant and not the other way around.

The right brain gets you into spirit and sees the wholeness of everything. Going into your right brain is like changing the channel, raising your vibration and bringing in the music of life. I know in writing this book my left brain kicked in and I felt blocked at times and I procrastinated. I would make all kinds of excuses why I couldn't sit down and write. Once I got myself settled down without the mind talk and started with just a few words the writing started to flow. I would tell myself, "You only have to write for a couple of minutes." This satisfied the left brain and allowed me to start writing. Once I began I was in the timeless right brain and I forgot the time. The key is to get you in the right brain.

Another good way to tap into the right brain is by journaling for fifteen minutes in the morning. This will satisfy the left brain. Just write down anything on your mind, rattle off things like: I have to empty the garbage, or dear God give me the answers to my prayers, or thank you for my blessings, or I don't know what to write or keep writing I don't know what to write. You get the picture……you don't have to keep what you write unless it is something you want to keep. If I am journaling for information it is one thing but if I am journaling to empty my left brain, then I toss it. Do this for fifteen minutes in the morning and by doing this you have satisfied the left brain with its constant rambling. This allows the right brain to switch on during the day giving you answers and opening you up to your creativity.

Do you ever notice how sometimes when you are driving you lose time and you discover answers. That is because when you are driving your left brain gets bored and your right brain switches on. To learn more about this a good book to read is "The Artists Way" by Julia Cameron.

Years ago I took the class: Drawing on the Right Side of the Brain by Betty Edwards. She had us draw upside down. It didn't make sense to the left brain so it turned off allowing the right brain to switch on. What a difference in the drawing when the right brain switched on. The right brain sees the wholeness of things and perceives reality like it really is.

Ask your spirit what it would like to do. What do you love? Listen to that inner voice and make the time for yourself. This is earth school and it seems to go by so fast. Add fun into your life. When you feel happy it affects everyone around you in a wonderful, wonderful way. I love that saying "I'm worth it". Try saying it and it will put a smile on your face.

I am going to share a story of a dear client who I help years ago but I hold the memory of the experience as a treasure. She and her family had just moved backed to California after living in Japan for two years. She had two young daughters ages twelve and fourteen. She was concerned about them adjusting to their new environment and making new friends. She also was concerned that they spent too much time in their bedrooms after school instead of participating as a family when they got home.

I went to her family room which happened to be in the children and creativity area of her home. It had beautiful crisp white walls, which is a favorable color of this area. She had brought some of her furniture back from Japan which was a traditional 18th century mahogany style. She wanted me to incorporate new pieces in this room that worked with her existing furniture that were in other rooms of the home.

We both wanted to make this area whimsical and fun. So we choose an Island mahogany maritime British style of furniture to incorporate with her other pieces of furniture. It was a British classics style bringing in the romance of island living with motifs of pineapples, leaves, and Redding.

She also told me that the girls loved animals and nature. So I brought in accessories that consisted of a turtle lamp, a monkey tray table, a little rabbit statue, a bird cage, lots of green plants, and a beautiful picture of colorful tropical birds. It was magical!

I brought in different colors and textures of fabric for the cushy upholstery like orange leather, a tropical print, an animal print and a luscious green.

It was an immediate success. When the girls came home from school they wanted to be in the family room instead of immediately going to their rooms. Her daughters were so happy with the family room they wanted me to do their bedrooms.

For their individual bedrooms I had each of the girls choose their favorite colors. They choose pastel colors of pink and violet.

We made sure the bed in each room was comfortable and suited for their individual tastes. The type of bed in which your child sleeps affects their growth. So to reap the best benefits the mother had me put in the best quality bed.

I also knew that in placing the bed for a child there are two areas of the room that are favorable. I always make sure with my clients that from the door you see the foot of the bed because this is placing your child that is sleeping in a commanding position.

Also if possible, it is important to place the bed of the child in the child's area of the room and in this case I was able to do so. By doing this and by placing the bed in the children's area it gives the child strength, intelligence, and energy.

Both daughters loved country French furniture and we had them pick out their own pieces. They each choose different pieces with an antique white finish. This with the different color themes, fabrics, and accessories for their bedrooms they both had their totally own look. The mother told me soon after we finished their bedrooms both daughters started having sleep overs with their new friends and their grades also started improving. When children love their environments everything seems like more fun. And life becomes richer.

To get in touch with your own inner child and bring joy and creativity into your life treat this area of your home. Place some fun pictures of the activities in this area you would like to be involved in. If you want to start dancing put a picture up of people dancing.

Start bringing in the energy of what you want to bring into your life. Bring in the things that bring you joy. I had a client who wanted to start painting again. So we brought out her easel and paint and put them in the creativity area. As soon as we did that, her whole face lit up. I had another client who wanted to start making jewelry. We set up the area in her home with all the tools she needed for jewelry making like beads, and jewels etc. She immediately got excited and now sells her jewelry in the store where she works and loves it. She is always creating a new piece of jewelry which brings her joy. She made me a pair of beautiful Feng Shui earrings. I love them and it makes me smile when I put them on.

When you are being creative you are one with your authentic self, you will be able to feel the very essence of life run through your blood, and you will be filled with joy! It is infectious!

Do something out of the norm that you have always wanted to do but would never think of doing.

I remember years ago when I was younger I was invited after work to go to an African drumming dancing class. I had never danced that way before and I didn't know if I would be comfortable. I ignored my fears and I went anyway and danced to the sound of the drums and heartbeat. It was one of the best experiences I have ever had in dancing. It was so much fun! I will never forget it. Just thinking of the experience makes me smile.

You want to address the children and creativity area when you feel creatively blocked and want to be more creative, when you are working on a creative project, when you have employees that need creativity in their work, when you want to improve the well-being and progress of your children, or when you want to explore your inner child.

The Angels to Call Upon for This Area

Call upon Archangel Metatron to help you with children that are sensitive. He will show you that all is possible for you and the children you care about. Call upon him especially if your life purpose involves helping and teaching children. He will help you with your natural talents and interests. If you allow it he will help you to develop a deeper spiritual path to higher creativity. He will help you discover and recover your creative self. His aura is green with pink strips. And his related crystal is watermelon tourmaline.

The next Archangel is Archangel Gabriel. She will help you nurture your children and your inner child. She will help you nurture your inner child with as much attention and love that is possible. She will help you rediscover your creative side. Work with her and the creativity will flow. Gabriel's aura is copper and the related crystal is citrine.

The next angel is Radueriel: the angel of artistic inspiration and creativity. Call upon him to bring out the natural talent residing in your soul. He will help you see the beauty that fills your soul, which must be allowed expression. He will help you get in touch with that inner magical child that is free and loves to create. What you create is a catharsis for you, allowing you to release and get into spirit. He will help you use your talent in whatever you feel it is best expressed. Your art will be an expression of the triumph of the human spirit. Your spirit and the spirit of those around you will be lifted in joy. Angel Radueriel has a silver aura and silver wings. Wear anything silver and invoke his assistance.

Meditation for the Inner Child

Put you in a relaxed position, either sitting or lying down. Close your eyes. Relax your feet, your ankles, your calves, your knees, you thighs, and your buttocks area. Relax your body up through your trunk, arms, fingers, neck, and head.

Now connect with the magnetic power of the earth. Draw the earth energy up into your feet, up your body, feel it surrounding your heart and reaching out into the universe, expanding in all directions. Take in a deep breath, breathing in love, and exhale, releasing all negativity. Now go to your room inside your heart, it is your sanctuary........

You are about the age of five. You listen to your inner child and you hear what he or she has to say. You tell your inner child that they are safe and much loved. Today you want the both of you to have fun...... You then begin to see or feel a heavenly spirit approaching..... She is fairy-like .... Emanating light....... It is Tinker.......

She is going to take the both of you to the magical land where children rule, play, have fun, and are creative.

You take the hand of your inner child and follow Tinker's light. You both soon arrive at the magical island where you feel the magic in the air. This is where you can fully embrace life and be as creative as you like.

She instructs you to go to a huge old closet. She tells you to open the closet door and for the both of you to walk into it. Once you step inside you find yourself in a room full of magical clothes. You begin putting some of the clothes on. You become creative and realize you can become anything/anyone you'd like.

You are transformed and you see yourself in the mirror all dressed up in the outfit of your choice. It is so fun and exciting and you feel yourself become that person. You know that almost everything you truly need or want is here for the asking. You know you only need to believe that it is so, truly desire it, and be willing to accept it.

You love the costume of your choice and you look at yourself in the mirror again and again in amazement........... You feel yourself transformed into this new reality ...... You are so excited..... It is so fun........ You marvel at your new appearance. You light with joy!

You and your inner child play for a while.........and when you feel it is time for you to leave you find yourself back the huge closet door. Before you return the costumes you look in the mirror one more time. You then put the clothes back in the magical closet and walk back through the huge closet door .... Once you are out of the closet Tinker arrives and takes you back where she found you....... She tells you.... You can come back to this place at any time. You and your inner child can just call upon her. You both say goodbye to her. You give your inner child a big hug and tell them what a wonderful time you had with them .... You say goodbye with gratitude.......

You slowly bring yourself back into your body and you begin to feel its sensations again. At the count of three you will be back, one, coming back, two, wiggling your fingers, and your toes, three, opening your eyes and you are back.

Feng Shui Charts

On the next two pages you will see charts that were created by my dear friend Holly. They are tools to help you get organized in the different areas of your life.

Use the next steps list to write down your personal goals under each of the headings. Check off each goal as it is attained.

Use the personal Bagua and write down what you want to manifest in the different areas of your life. Write down the physical enhancements you want to place in the different areas to assist in for your wishes to manifest.

After the charts will be the answers to the Feng Shui Questions in Chapter One. This will be followed by a Feng Shui Vision Board exercise. Enjoy!

NEXT STEPS

HEALTH & BALANCE			

CAREER			

SPIRITUAL & PERSONAL DEVELOPMENT			

FAMILY & COMMUNITY			

WEALTH			

FAME			

RELATIONSHIPS			

CHILDREN & CREATIVITY			

HELPFUL FRIENDS & TRAVEL			

PERSONAL BAGUA FOR: _____

WEALTH & ABUNDANCE	FAME	RELATIONSHIPS
• • • •	• • • •	• • • •
FAMILY	HEALTH & BALANCE	CHILDREN & CREATIVITY
• • • •	• • • •	• • • •
SELF-DEV. & SPIRITUALITY	CAREER	HELFUL FRIENDS & TRAVEL
• • • •	• • • •	• • • •

Feng Shui Answers

Feng Shui (pronounced Fung Shway)

A Chinese term meaning "wind + water practiced for over Three Thousand Years

Feng Shui, literally means wind and water. It is rapidly becoming a standard practice for creating the ideal environment in which to live and work.

Elements

Metal   Wood   Water   Fire   Earth

What: The Chinese art of Placement

There is a Chinese saying.……..."If you want change in your life, move 27 things in your house".

There are three basic principles that form the foundation on which Feng Shui is built.

These principles define chi (energy around us)

1. Everything is alive
2. Everything is connected
3. Everything is changing

When: When to apply principles:

#1   Increase your prosperity

#2   Enhance your relationships

#3   Boost your health

#4   Upgrade your life in any way

Where: In the environment where you live, work, your car, and places you stay when you travel.

How: Balance the yin and the yang

Mixing the five elements just right metal, water, wood, fire, and earth

Locating your treasures – How to use the Bagua Map

Bagua areas   Bagua enhancements

Why: Bring people back into a healthful balance

A Feng Shui Vision Board

ABUNDANCE & PROSPERITY Purples, reds, and blues	ILLUMINATION FAME & REPUTATION reds	LOVE & REPUTATION Whites, pinks, and reds
FOUNDATION & FAMILY Blues, and greens	HEALTH & WELL BEING Yellow and earth tones	CREATIVITY & CHILDREN White and pastels
SKILL & INNER KNOWLEDGE Black, blues and greens	CAREER & LIFE'S JOURNEY Black and dark tones	HELPFUL PEOPLE & Travel White, grey, and black

Expressing yourself creatively is one of the most powerful ways to activate joy, enthusiasm and participation in life. Make a Vision Board in the form of the Bagua.

Write in the different Bagua areas on poster paper and have a pile of magazines you can pull pictures out of.

Do a brief breathing exercise to get yourself out of your head and into your heart. Call in your Higher self.

Your soul does not communicate with words but pictures. Your soul knows your heart's desire. Take magazines and pull the pictures out that bring you excitement. You do not have to use all pictures but start working with them with your Bagua. If possible get some Elmer's Rubber Cement. It is easy to glue the pictures or picture in the desired space. Remember you are creating your new reality. Get out of your head and into your heart. Do not give yourself too much time to think. Once you have your pictures give yourself 30-45 minutes to complete the Board.

When you are done with the Vision Board get together with a friend and share your life using the Bagua map. **Pretend** you haven't seen each other in a year and share what you **have done** and what you **have been doing** using the Vision Board. Go through each area of your life. Using your imagination is a powerful tool. (You fake it until you make it).

You will be living your future in the present with the spoken word. The spoken word is very powerful and goes into the subconscious and the subconscious is your connection to the divine source and it always reaches its goal.

If you can't get together with a friend do the exercise in the mirror and talk with yourself.

May you activate joy, abundance, Love, and participation in life with many Blessings!

Serafina

About the Author

Serafina Krupp Feng Shui, Angels, Author Serafina is a renowned Master Teacher, Interior Designer, and practitioner in Angelic Feng Shui and has been exploring the art and science of Feng Shui since she discovered it while she was studying for a master's degree in Interior Design. Her mission is to empower men and women to create the spaces they want to live and work in and to create enlightened changes in their lives. Through the practice and teachings of Angelic Feng Shui, Serafina brings balance to the mind, body and spirit within the interior and exterior spaces of the world around us.

Serafina first studied Feng Shui under Lillian Garnier of The Lotus Institute and the author of "Face Reading in Chinese Medicine", who exposed her to the Western thought of Feng Shui. Her second Master Teacher was Robin Yoshida, a Visionary Holistic Life Coach & Energy Medicine Specialist from whom Serafina learned the healing aspects of Feng Shui. With this unique background, she has developed a highly effective system of Angelic Feng Shui that fits with any type of living environment.

Today, Serafina brings forth the practice of Angelic Feng Shui and Interior Design at an understandable level with the teachings, passion and sacredness of the cultures of the past and the sophistication, maturity, and needs of her clients and students in today's modern world. Her passion is to effect positive changes in one's lifestyle, surroundings, relationships and financial returns.

For more info on Serafina and her private services contact www.serafinaonline.com Serafina@serafinaonline.com

Testimonials

"As an interior designer, you have a great sense of style. You were able to incorporate new items with my existing decor and to achieve an environment that our family loves. Serafina you are incredibly personable, and enthusiasm to each meeting we had. Your patience and concern for the whole families input and feelings, made working with you a pleasurable experience. I look forward being with you in the future."

Elizabeth Simms
Newport Beach, California

"My clients were <u>so</u> impressed by how you quickly sized up the rooms and made the appropriate changes. Your services had significant financial value to raising the bar on our client's property."

Ros Essner
Real Estate Out of the Box
Huntington Beach, California

"You made our day, Serafina. We love meeting you and were touched deeply by you and your generous, angelic spirit."

Barbara and Jerry Silverstein
Mission Viejo, California

"I have hated my living room for the last six years we've lived in this house. Serafina was able to transform the space through arrangement and color. Now, I love to just sit in the living room because I feel so peaceful and good there."

Holly Kruger
Campbell Real Estate
Huntington Beach, California

"Thank you Serafina for the magic you sprinkled on my home and me. You worked wonders on my home and brought your magic to the Abundance Retreat for Women once again. Bless you for your skills and talents."

Dr. Carol Most